D1716582

THE U.S. JUSTICE SYSTEM

THE U.S. JUSTICE SYSTEM

Ellen Dupont

Foreword by Manny Gomez, Esq.

MASON CREST

Mason Crest
450 Parkway Drive, Suite D
Broomall, PA 19008
www.masoncrest.com

Printed and bound in the United States of America

First printing
9 8 7 6 5 4 3 2 1

Series ISBN: 978-1-4222-3469-3
Hardcover ISBN: 978-1-4222-3488-4
ebook ISBN: 978-1-4222-8415-5

Library of Congress Cataloging-in-Publication Data on file with the Library of Congress

Developed and Produced by Print Matters Productions, Inc. (www.printmattersinc.com)

Developmental Editor: Amy Hackney Blackwell
Cover and Interior Design: Tom Carling, Carling Design Inc.

> **Note on Statistics:** While every effort has been made to provide the most up-to-date government statistics, the Department of Justice and other agencies compile new data at varying intervals, sometimes as much as ten years. Agency publications are often based on data compiled from a period ending a year or two before the publication date.

CONTENTS

KEY ICONS TO LOOK FOR:

Text-Dependent Questions: These questions send the reader back to the text for more careful attention to the evidence presented there.

Words to Understand: These words with their easy-to-understand definitions will increase the reader's understanding of the text while building vocabulary skills.

Series Glossary of Key Terms: This back-of-the-book glossary contains terminology used throughout this series. Words found here increase the reader's ability to read and comprehend higher-level books and articles in this field.

Research Projects: Readers are pointed toward areas of further inquiry connected to each chapter. Suggestions are provided for projects that encourage deeper research and analysis.

Sidebars: This boxed material within the main text allows readers to build knowledge, gain insights, explore possibilities, and broaden their perspectives by weaving together additional information to provide realistic and holistic perspectives.

FOREWORD

Experience Counts

Detecting crime and catching lawbreakers is a very human endeavor. Even the best technology has to be guided by human intelligence to be used effectively. If there's one truth from my thirty years in law enforcement and security, it's trust your gut.

When I started on the police force, I learned from older officers and from experience what things to look for, what traits, characteristics, or indicators lead to somebody who is about to commit a crime or in the process of committing one. You learn from experience. The older generation of law enforcement teaches the younger generation, and then, if you're good, you pick up your own little nuances as to what bad guys are doing.

In my early work, I specialized in human intelligence, getting informants to tell me what was happening on the street. Most of the time it was people I arrested that I then "flipped" to inform me where the narcotics were being stored, how they were being delivered, how they were being sold, the patterns, and other crucial details.

A good investigator has to be organized since evidence must be presented in a legally correct way to hold up in court. Evidence from a crime scene has to have a perfect chain of custody. Any mishandling turns the evidence to fruits of a poisonous tree.

At my company, MG Security Services, which provides private security to corporate and individual clients in the New York area, we are always trying to learn and to pass on that learning to our security officers in the field.

Certainly, the field of detection has evolved dramatically in the last 100 years. Recording devices have been around for a long time; it's just that now they've gotten really good. Today, a pen can be a video recording device; whereas in the old days it would have been a large box with two wheels. The equipment was awkward and not too subtle: it would be eighty degrees out, you'd be sweating in a raincoat, and the box would start clicking.

The forensic part of detection is very high-tech these days, especially with DNA coming into play in the last couple of decades. A hundred years ago, fingerprinting revolutionized detective work; the next breakthrough is facial recognition. We have recently discovered that the arrangement of facial features (measured as nodes) is unique to each individual. No two people on the planet have the exact same configuration of nodes. Just as it took decades to build out the database of known fingerprints, facial recognition is a work in progress. We will see increasing collection of facial data when people obtain official identification. There are privacy concerns, but we're working them out. Facial recognition will be a centerpiece of future detection and prevention efforts.

Technology offers law enforcement important tools that we're learning to apply strategically. Algorithms already exist that allow retailers to signal authorities when someone makes a suspicious purchase—known bomb-making ingredients, for example. Cities are loaded with sensors to detect the slightest trace of nuclear, biological, or chemical materials that pose a threat to the public. And equipment nested on streetlights in New York City can triangulate the exact block where a gun was fired.

Now none of this does anything constructive without well-trained professionals ready and able to put the information to use. The tools evolve, but what doesn't evolve is human intelligence.

Law enforcement as a community is way ahead in fighting street and violent crime than the newer challenges of cybercrime and terrorism. Technology helps, but it all goes back to human intelligence. There is no substitute for the cop on the street, knowing what is going on in the neighborhood, knowing who the players are. When the cop has quality informants inside gangs, he or she knows when there's going to be a hit, a drug drop, or an illicit transaction. The human intelligence comes first; then you can introduce the technology, such as hidden cameras or other surveillance.

The twin challenges for domestic law enforcement are gangs and guns. Gangs are a big problem in this country. That's a cultural and social phenomenon that law enforcement has not yet found an effective way to counteract. We need to study that more diligently. If we're successful in getting rid of the gangs, or at least diluting them, we will have come a long way in fighting violent crime. But guns are the main issue. You look at England, a first-world country of highly educated people that strictly regulates guns, and the murder rate is minimal.

When it comes to cybercrime, we're woefully behind. That's simply because we hire people for the long term, and their skills get old. You have a twenty-five-year-old who's white-hot now, but guess what? In five years that skill set is lost. Hackers, on the other hand, are young people who tend to evolve fast. They learn so much more than their older law-enforcement counterparts and are able to penetrate systems too easily. The Internet was not built with the security of private users in mind. It is like a house with no door locks, and now we're trying to figure ways to secure the house. It was done kind of backward. Nobody really thought that it was going to be this wide-open door to criminal activity.

We need to change the equation for cybercriminals. Right now the chances are they won't get caught; cybercrime offers criminals huge benefit at very little cost. Law enforcement needs to recruit young people who can match skills with the criminals. We also need to work closely with foreign governments and agencies to better identify, deter, and apprehend cybercriminals. We need to make examples of them.

Improving our cybercrime prevention means a lot more talent, a lot more resources, a lot more hands-on collaboration with countries on the outskirts—Russia, China, even Israel. These are the countries that are constantly trying to penetrate our cyberspace. And even if we are able to identify the person overseas, we still need the cooperation of the overseas government and law enforcement to help us find and apprehend the person. Electrical grids are extremely vulnerable to cyber attacks. Utilities built long before the Internet need engineering retrofits to make them better able to withstand attacks.

As with cybercrime, efforts against terrorism must be coordinated to be effective. Communication is crucial among all levels of law enforcement, from local law enforcement and national agencies sharing information—in both directions—to a similar international flow of information among different countries' governments and national bureaus.

In the U.S., since 9/11, the FBI and local law enforcement now share a lot more information with each other locally and nationally. Internationally, as well, we are sharing more information with Interpol and other intelligence and law enforcement agencies throughout the world to be able to better detect, identify, and prevent criminal activity.

When it comes to terrorism, we also need to ramp up our public relations. Preventing terror attacks takes more than a military response. We need to address this culture of death with our own Internet media campaign and 800 numbers to make it easy for people to reach out to law enforcement and help build the critical human infrastructure. Without people, there are no leads—people on the inside of a criminal enterprise are essential to directing law enforcement resources effectively, telling you when to listen, where to watch, and which accounts to check.

In New York City, the populace is well aware of the "see something, say something" campaign. Still, we need to do more. More people need to speak up. Again, it comes down to trusting your instincts. If someone seems a little off to you, find a law enforcement representative and share your perception. Listen to your gut. Your gut will always tell you: there's something hinky going on here. Human beings have a sixth sense that goes back to our caveman days when animals used to hunt us. So take action, talk to law enforcement when something about a person makes you uneasy or you feel something around you isn't right.

We have to be prepared not just on the prevention side but in terms of responses. Almost every workplace conducts a fire drill at least once a year. We need to do the same with active-shooter drills. Property managers today may even have their own highly trained active-shooter teams, ready to be on site within minutes of any attack.

We will never stop crime, but we can contain the harm it causes. The coordinated efforts of law enforcement, an alert and well-trained citizenry, and the smart use of DNA, facial profiles, and fingerprinting will go a long way toward reducing the number and severity of terror events.

Be it the prevention of street crime or cybercrime, gang violence or terrorism, sharing information is essential. Only then can we put our technology to good use. People are key to detection and prevention. Without the human element, I like to say a camera's going to take a pretty picture of somebody committing a crime.

Law enforcement must strive to attract qualified people with the right instincts, team-sensibility, and work ethic. At the end of the day, there's no hunting like the hunting of man. It's a thrill; it's a rush; and that to me is law enforcement in its purest form.

MANNY GOMEZ, Esq.

President of MG Security Services,

Chairman of the National Law Enforcement Association,

former FBI Special Agent,

U.S. Marine, and NYPD Sergeant

We the People

of the United States, in order to form a more perfect Union, establish Justice, insure domestic Tranquility, provide for the common Defense, promote the general Welfare, and secure the Blessings of Liberty to ourselves and our Posterity, do ordain and establish this Constitution for the United States of America.

Article. I.

Section. 1. All legislative Powers herein granted shall be vested in a Congress of the United States, which shall consist of a Senate and House of Representatives.

Section. 2. The House of Representatives shall be composed of Members chosen every second Year by the People of the several States, and the Electors in each State shall have the Qualifications requisite for Electors of the most numerous Branch of the State Legislature.

No Person shall be a Representative who shall not have attained to the Age of twenty five Years, and been seven Years a Citizen of the United States, and who shall not, when elected, be an Inhabitant of that State in which he shall be chosen.

Representatives and direct Taxes shall be apportioned among the several States which may be included within this Union, according to their respective Numbers, which shall be determined by adding to the whole Number of free Persons, including those bound to Service for a Term of Years, and excluding Indians not taxed, three fifths of all other Persons. The actual Enumeration shall be made within three Years after the first Meeting of the Congress of the United States, and within every subsequent Term of ten Years, in such Manner as they shall by Law direct. The Number of Representatives shall not exceed one for every thirty Thousand, but each State shall have at Least one Representative; and until such enumeration shall be made, the State of New Hampshire shall be entitled to chuse three, Massachusetts eight, Rhode Island and Providence Plantations one, Connecticut five, New York six, New Jersey four, Pennsylvania eight, Delaware one, Maryland six, Virginia ten, North Carolina five, South Carolina five, and Georgia three.

When vacancies happen in the Representation from any State, the Executive Authority thereof shall issue Writs of Election to fill such Vacancies.

The House of Representatives shall chuse their Speaker and other Officers; and shall have the sole Power of Impeachment.

Section. 3. The Senate of the United States shall be composed of two Senators from each State, chosen by the Legislature thereof, for six Years; and each Senator shall have one Vote.

Immediately after they shall be assembled in Consequence of the first Election, they shall be divided as equally as may be into three Classes. The Seats of the Senators of the first Class shall be vacated at the Expiration of the second Year, of the second Class at the Expiration of the fourth Year, and of the third Class at the Expiration of the sixth Year, so that one third may be chosen every second Year; and if Vacancies happen by Resignation, or otherwise, during the Recess of the Legislature of any State, the Executive thereof may make temporary Appointments until the next Meeting of the Legislature, which shall then fill such Vacancies.

No Person shall be a Senator who shall not have attained to the Age of thirty Years, and been nine Years a Citizen of the United States, and who shall not, when elected, be an Inhabitant of that State for which he shall be chosen.

The Vice President of the United States shall be President of the Senate, but shall have no Vote, unless they be equally divided.

The Senate shall chuse their other Officers, and also a President pro tempore, in the Absence of the Vice President, or when he shall exercise the Office of President of the United States.

~~~~~~~~~

The Senators and Representatives before mentioned, and the Members of the several State Legislatures, and all executive and judicial Officers, both of the United States and of the several States, shall be bound by Oath or Affirmation, to support this Constitution; but no religious Test shall ever be required as a Qualification to any Office or public Trust under the United States.

Article. VII.

The Ratification of the Conventions of nine States, shall be sufficient for the Establishment of this Constitution between the States so ratifying the Same.

The Word, "the," being interlined between the seventh and eighth Lines of the first Page, The Word "Thirty" being partly written on an Erasure in the fifteenth Line of the first Page. The Words "is tried" being interlined between the thirty second and thirty third Lines of the first Page and the Word "the" being interlined between the forty third and forty fourth Lines of the second Page.

Done

in Convention by the Unanimous Consent of the States present the Seventeenth Day of September in the Year of our Lord one thousand seven hundred and Eighty seven and of the Independence of the United States of America the Twelfth. In Witness whereof We have hereunto subscribed our Names.

Attest William Jackson Secretary

G°. Washington
Presidt and deputy from Virginia

Delaware
Geo: Read
Gunning Bedford jun
John Dickinson
Richard Bassett
Jaco: Broom

Maryland
James McHenry
Dan of St Thos. Jenifer
Danl Carroll

Virginia
John Blair
James Madison Jr.

North Carolina
Wm. Blount
Richd. Dobbs Spaight
Hu Williamson

J. Rutledge
Charles Cotesworth Pinckney

New Hampshire
John Langdon
Nicholas Gilman

Massachusetts
Nathaniel Gorham
Rufus King

Connecticut
Wm. Saml. Johnson
Roger Sherman

New York
Alexander Hamilton

New Jersey
Wil: Livingston
David Brearley
Wm. Paterson
Jona: Dayton

Pennsylvania
B Franklin
Thomas Mifflin
Robt. Morris

CHAPTER I

UNDERSTANDING THE CONSTITUTION

Words to Understand

Appeal: referral of a case to a higher court for review

Certificate of certiorari: a document which a losing party files with the Supreme Court, asking the Supreme Court to review the decision of a lower Court, it includes a list of the parties, a statement of the facts of the case, and arguments as to why the Court should grant the writ

Petition: a formal written request made to an official person or organized body

Precedent: something done or said that serves as an example or rule to authorize or justify a subsequent act of similar kind

AT THE END OF THE REVOLUTIONARY WAR, THE 13 COLONIES WON THEIR FREEDOM FROM GREAT BRITAIN AND BECAME 13 STATES, BUT IT WAS HARD FOR THEM TO WORK TOGETHER AS A COUNTRY. THE ARTICLES OF CONFEDERATION UNITED THE 13 STATES, BUT EACH STATE WAS STILL ESSENTIALLY INDEPENDENT. THE STATES OFTEN ACTED IN THEIR OWN BEST INTERESTS AND NOT FOR THE GOOD OF THE COUNTRY. FOR EXAMPLE, SOME STATES TAXED GOODS COMING IN FROM OTHER STATES, WHICH MADE TRADE BETWEEN STATES DIFFICULT.

The original Constitution was signed in September 1787 by 39 delegates (plus one in absentia), laying the legal foundations for the United States. It is displayed at the National Archive in Washington, D.C. At the end of each day, the display is lowered into a vault for safekeeping.

People realized that in order to function effectively as a country, the Articles of Confederation would have to be revised. In 1787, Alexander Hamilton organized a national convention, and delegates came to Philadelphia from all the states except Rhode Island. The people of Rhode Island did not want a strong national government that might interfere in their affairs. People who felt this way were known as antifederalists. The federalists, on the other hand, wanted a country with a strong central government.

When the delegates began to discuss what to add to the Articles of Confederation, they soon realized that what was needed was a completely new document—the Constitution. The Constitution created a federal system of government in which some of the power rests with the national government and some powers stay with the state governments. The Constitution thus enabled the states to work with each other while still protecting their rights and independence.

To achieve this balance among national government, state governments, and individuals, the Constitution outlined a new kind of government based on a separation of powers and a system of checks and balances. The power of the government was divided into three parts: the executive branch, which is led by the president and enforces the laws; the legislative branch, which makes laws in the Congress; and the judicial branch, which interprets the laws through the courts. As a result, none of these three branches can ever gain the upper hand over the other two.

The Assembly Room, located in Philadelphia, Pennsylvania, held many monumental moments in American history, including the signing of the Constitution. The room is open to visitors each day during museum hours.

Leading delegates at the National Convention discuss the drafting of the Constitution in Philadelphia in 1787. In all, 55 delegates attended the Constitutional Convention sessions, but only 40 actually signed the Constitution. The delegates ranged in age from Jonathan Dayton, aged 26, to Benjamin Franklin, aged 81, who was so infirm that he had to be carried to sessions in a sedan chair.

In 1787 Alexander Hamilton organized a national convention to revise the Articles of Confederation. But when the delegates arrived in Philadelphia they decided that a new document was needed—and so the U.S. Constitution was born.

The Magna Carta

When King John ruled England, he kept raising taxes and forcing his knights to fight in fruitless foreign wars. The knights decided that they wanted him to run the country more fairly, so in 1215, they wrote a document, the Magna Carta (meaning "Great Charter" in Latin), and made him sign it. It gave the knights certain rights and limited the king's power, ensuring that he obeyed the law. Written by noblemen, the Magna Carta talks only about the rights of the nobility, but later on, people came to believe that everyone in a democracy should have rights, too.

The Constitution took a long time to write. Every word was hotly debated, and compromises were hammered out in order to produce a document on which everyone could agree. Finally, the delegates signed the Constitution. Then it had to be ratified by nine states to become law.

The Bill Of Rights

Most states agreed to the Constitution, but North Carolina and Rhode Island would not ratify it until a Bill of Rights was added. They wanted to make sure that the government did not have too much power over people. The first 10 amendments added to the Constitution are known as the Bill of Rights.

At the time that the Constitution and the Bill of Rights were written, the colonists remembered what it had been like when the British ruled the country. They knew how it felt to be forbidden to speak their minds or to practice their chosen religion. They knew that a powerful government can be unfair and ruthless, and that without written rights, there was no guarantee that the government would treat them fairly.

The Bill of Rights guarantees the people certain rights. It ensures that even though the government is large and powerful and the individual is small and weak in comparison, the government's power is limited. The rights guaranteed in the Bill of Rights include freedom of speech, religion, and the press; the right to get together; the right to **petition** the government; and the right to bear arms.

The Bill of Rights also made sure that even someone charged with a crime had rights. The Fifth Amendment gives anyone accused of a crime the right to due process of law (fair treatment under the law). It also gives the accused the right to remain silent, guaranteeing that the state cannot make anyone testify against himself. It also says that no one can be tried twice for the same crime, sometimes called "double jeopardy." Under the Fourth Amendment, individuals are given protection against unreasonable searches and seizures, forbidding government officials from searching houses or taking property without a court's permission.

Other amendments guarantee the accused a fair, speedy, and public trial. The last two amendments make it clear that any rights not explicitly given in the Bill of Rights belong either to the states or to the individual. Privacy, for example, is not mentioned in the Bill of Rights, but the Supreme Court has ruled that it is one of the "unenumerated" rights meant by the Ninth Amendment and, as such, it is protected by the Constitution.

Bill of Rights

Congress of the United States,

begun and held at the City of New York, on

Wednesday, the fourth of March, one thousand seven hundred and eighty nine.

The Conventions of a number of the States having, at the time of their adopting the Constitution, expressed a desire, in order to prevent misconstruction or abuse of its powers, that further declaratory and restrictive clauses should be added: And as extending the ground of public confidence in the Government, will best insure the beneficent ends of its institution:

Resolved, by the SENATE and HOUSE of REPRESENTATIVES of the UNITED STATES of AMERICA in Congress assembled, two thirds of both Houses concurring, That the following Articles be proposed to the Legislatures of the several States, as Amendments to the Constitution of the United States; all, or any of which articles, when ratified by three fourths of the said Legislatures, to be valid to all intents and purposes, as part of the said Constitution, viz.

Articles in addition to, and Amendment of the Constitution of the United States of America, proposed by Congress, and ratified by the Legislatures of the several States, pursuant to the fifth Article of the Original Constitution.

Article the first ...... After the first enumeration required by the first Article of the Constitution, there shall be one Representative for every thirty thousand, until the number shall amount to one hundred, after which, the proportion shall be so regulated by Congress, that there shall be not less than one hundred Representatives, nor less than one Representative for every forty thousand persons, until the number of Representatives shall amount to two hundred, after which, the proportion shall be so regulated by Congress, that there shall not be less than two hundred Representatives, nor more than one Representative for every fifty thousand persons. [Not Ratified]

Article the second .... No law, varying the compensation for the services of the Senators and Representatives, shall take effect, until an election of Representatives shall have intervened. [Not Ratified]

Article the third .... Congress shall make no law respecting an establishment of religion, or prohibiting the free exercise thereof; or abridging the freedom of speech, or of the press; or the right of the people peaceably to assemble, and to petition the Government for a redress of grievances.

Article the fourth ..... A well regulated Militia, being necessary to the security of a free State, the right of the people to keep and bear Arms, shall not be infringed.

Article the fifth .... No Soldier shall, in time of peace, be quartered in any house, without the consent of the owner, nor in time of war, but in a manner to be prescribed by law.

Article the sixth ...... The right of the people to be secure in their persons, houses, papers, and effects, against unreasonable searches and seizures, shall not be violated, and no Warrants shall issue but upon probable cause, supported by oath or affirmation, and particularly describing the place to be searched, and the persons or things to be seized.

Article the seventh ... No person shall be held to answer for a capital, or otherwise infamous crime, unless on a presentment or indictment of a grand jury, except in cases arising in the land or Naval forces, or in the Militia, when in actual service in time of War or public danger; nor shall any person be subject for the same offence to be twice put in jeopardy of life or limb; nor shall be compelled in any criminal case, to be a witness against himself, nor be deprived of life, liberty, or property, without due process of law; nor shall private property be taken for public use without just compensation.

Article the eighth ..... In all criminal prosecutions, the accused shall enjoy the right to a speedy and public trial, by an impartial jury of the State and district wherein the crime shall have been committed, which district shall have been previously ascertained by law, and to be informed of the nature and cause of the accusation; to be confronted with the witnesses against him; to have compulsory process for obtaining witnesses in his favor, and to have the assistance of counsel for his defence.

Article the ninth ...... In suits at common law, where the value in controversy shall exceed twenty dollars, the right of trial by jury shall be preserved, and no fact, tried by a jury, shall be otherwise re-examined in any Court of the United States, than according to the rules of the common law.

Article the tenth ...... Excessive bail shall not be required, nor excessive fines imposed, nor cruel and unusual punishments inflicted.

Article the eleventh .. The enumeration in the Constitution, of certain rights, shall not be construed to deny or disparage others retained by the people.

Article the twelfth .... The powers not delegated to the United States by the Constitution, nor prohibited by it to the States, are reserved to the States respectively, or to the people.

ATTEST,

Frederick Augustus Muhlenberg, Speaker of the House of Representatives.

John Adams, Vice-President of the United States, and President of the Senate.

John Beckley, Clerk of the House of Representatives.

Sam. A. Otis Secretary of the Senate.

The Bill of Rights constitutes the first 10 amendments added to the United States Constitution.

First president of the United States George Washington made sure that the place of the National Guard was enshrined in the U.S. Constitution. Here, members of the National Guard provide security at Ground Zero, following the attacks on the World Trade Center, September 11, 2001.

No One Is Above the Law

The Constitution and the Bill of Rights together ensure that the law itself is more powerful than any person or organization. Even the president or a powerful organization like the FBI cannot deny people their rights. In addition, the most powerful people and organizations in the land are subject to the same laws as everyone else, so if they break the law, they, too, can be tried and punished.

The framers of the Constitution also created a way to amend the constitution. It is now more than 200 years since the Constitution was ratified, and in addition to the 10 amendments that make up the Bill of Rights, there have been 17 amendments. Some of the most famous are Amendment 13, which abolished slavery, and Amendment 19, which gave women the right to vote. The most recently ratified was Amendment 27, added in 1992. This amendment, which prohibits any law changing the salary of Congress from taking effect until the start of the next term of office for Representatives, was initially proposed in 1789, but did not receive support from the required number of states for 202 years.

The Constitution is the most basic, fundamental law in the United States and it cannot be contradicted by any other law. But sometimes it is not easy to know exactly what the Constitution means. Sometimes, the wording is unclear, or there might be terms whose meanings are open to debate. For example, the Second Amendment of the Bill of Rights says, "A well regulated Militia, being necessary to the security of a free State, the right of the people to keep and bear Arms, shall not be infringed." Does this mean everyone is allowed to have a gun, or just people in a well-regulated militia? And if so, what is "a well-regulated militia"? Arguments about America's gun laws continue to this day.

The Supreme Court

Even when the Constitution was first written, people debated what it meant. The controversy continues today as we try to apply the Constitution to the world we live in now. It is the job of the Supreme Court to decide what the Constitution means. The Supreme Court is empowered under Article III of the Constitution to hear cases about the Constitution, the laws of the United States, and treaties made by the U.S. government, as well as certain other specific kinds of cases. The Supreme Court also hears cases for which a petition "for certification to **appeal**" has been granted by it. This means the Supreme Court chooses which cases it wants to hear. Many cases are appealed to the Supreme Court, but only about one percent are heard. Those cases are granted a **certificate of certiorari** by the Court. These cases come from the appellate, state, and federal courts. Because it is the highest court in the land, the Supreme Court's decisions are final.

Today, a chief justice and eight associate justices sit on the Supreme Court. They are appointed by the president and approved by the Senate. The Senate does not automatically approve the president's appointments. In fact, on average, 20 percent of presidential nominees are rejected. The president usually chooses nominees who agree with the president's way of thinking. Presidents also like to preserve a balance on the court between the sexes, different races, and religions.

Once appointed, justices sit on the Supreme Court for life. This makes them independent of public and political opinion, which means they do not have to worry that they will lose their jobs if they make an unpopular decision. A Supreme Court justice can therefore sit on the court for many years. Just one example of many is Justice William O. Douglas, who was appointed by Franklin D. Roosevelt in 1939 and served until 1975. In his 36 years on the court, six presidents (Truman, Eisenhower, Kennedy, Johnson, Nixon, and Ford) held office.

Oliver Wendell Holmes (1841–1935) served on the U.S. Supreme Court for 30 years. He was nicknamed "the Great Dissenter" because he frequently disagreed with the majority of his conservative colleagues, particularly when they moved to dismantle social legislation.

A demonstrator shows his patriotism and support for the United States in front of the Supreme Court in Washington, D.C. in 2001. The Supreme Court was forced to convene at a different location for the first time since its opening in 1935 after anthrax was discovered in its offsite mailroom.

Although there are some cases that go straight to the Supreme Court, such as boundary disputes between states, most of the cases that they hear are those on appeal. If either side disagrees with the decision of a lower court based on a point of law, they have the right to appeal to a higher court. That court then reviews the decision and either upholds it (meaning the decision stands) or strikes it (meaning the decision is reversed). Appellate courts look at the legal reasoning of the lower court's decision, not at who is right or wrong.

The United States Supreme Court Justices sit for a group photo in 2010. They are (front row from left) Clarence Thomas, Antonin Scalia, John G. Roberts (Chief Justice), Anthony Kennedy, Ruth Bader Ginsburg; (back row from left) Sonia Sotomayor, Stephen Breyer, Samuel Alito, and Elena Kagan.

Marbury v. Madison

In this case, the Supreme Court created the principle of judicial review. This meant that it had the power to review laws made by the president or Congress and to invalidate any laws that the Court believed violated the Constitution.

On his last day in office, President John Adams appointed William Marbury as a judge. But the appointment papers were not filed. When the new president, Thomas Jefferson, came into office, he told Secretary of State James Madison (pictured) not to honor the appointment. Marbury therefore sued Madison. The case was heard in the Supreme Court in 1803. Although Marbury won the case in principle, he never became a judge. The case is historic, however, not because of what it decided about Marbury, but because of what it said about the jurisdiction, or power, of the Supreme Court.

John Marshall, the chief justice, wrote the decision, saying, "It is emphatically the province and duty of the judicial department to say what the law is." He said that since the Constitution is the supreme law, it is the Supreme Court's responsibility to interpret it and to resolve any conflict between state and federal law and the Constitution, thus creating the concept of judicial review.

The Court of Last Resort

The Supreme Court is the highest court in the land and, as such, is the court of last resort. This is the final appeal a case can have. Usually, the court decides which cases to hear based on what issues they think are important to Americans in general or to a particular group in society.

When a case comes before the Supreme Court, both sides write a legal summary, called a brief, explaining why the legal reasoning in the case was defective. They also submit all the documents and transcripts from the lower court. On the day the case is heard, the two sides each have 30 minutes to present their case. However, it is not just a time for the lawyers to make speeches; the justices ask them difficult legal questions.

Afterward, the justices discuss the case in private. When they enter the conference room, they shake hands to show that they are discussing the case in a spirit of friendliness. The chief justice takes charge. Six of the nine justices must take part in the discussion of the case. At the end, they vote on the case, and the majority rules. If the justices are tied, then the decision taken by the court below the Supreme Court stands.

After the vote has been taken, one of the justices writes an opinion explaining the decision. This is called the majority opinion. Sometimes, a justice will agree with the decision, but not with the reasoning behind it and will write a concurring opinion. The justices who did not agree with the majority can explain why in a dissenting opinion.

The process of writing the opinions is an important one. Sometimes, the arguments in the opinions are so persuasive that justices change their minds and change their vote, thus changing the court's decision. This is allowed at any time up to the announcement of the decision.

Supreme Court decisions are important, not just for the particular case, but for future cases, because they set a **precedent** and give lawyers an idea of how the justices might decide similar cases in the future. All of the Supreme Court's decisions put together make up constitutional law, the most basic and fundamental law in the United States.

The Bill Of Rights

AMENDMENT 1

Congress shall make no law respecting an establishment of religion, or prohibiting the free exercise thereof; or abridging the freedom of speech, or of the press; or the right of the people peaceably to assemble, and to petition the Government for a redress of grievances.

AMENDMENT 2

A well-regulated Militia, being necessary to the security of a free State, the right of the people to keep and bear Arms, shall not be infringed.

AMENDMENT 3

No Soldier shall, in time of peace, be quartered in any house, without the consent of the Owner, nor in time of war, but in a manner to be prescribed by law.

AMENDMENT 4

The right of the people to be secure in their persons, houses, papers, and effects, against unreasonable searches and seizures, shall not be violated, and no Warrants shall issue, but upon probable cause, supported by Oath or affirmation, and particularly describing the place to be searched, and the persons or things to be seized.

AMENDMENT 5

No person shall be held to answer for a capital, or otherwise infamous crime, unless on a presentment or indictment of a Grand Jury, except in cases arising in the land or naval forces, or in the Militia, when in actual service in time of War or public danger; nor shall any person be subject for the same offense to be a witness against himself; nor be deprived of life, liberty, or property, without due process of law; nor shall private property be taken for public use, without just compensation.

AMENDMENT 6

In all criminal prosecutions, the accused shall enjoy the right to a speedy and public trial, by an impartial jury of the State and district wherein the crime shall have been committed, which district shall have been previously ascertained by law, and to be informed of the nature and cause of the accusation; to be confronted with the witnesses against him; to have compulsory process for obtaining witnesses in his favor, and to have the Assistance of Counsel for his defense.

AMENDMENT 7

In Suits at common law, where the value in controversy shall exceed twenty dollars, the right of trial by jury shall be preserved, and no fact tried by a jury, shall be otherwise re-examined in any Court of the United States, than according to the rules of the common law.

AMENDMENT 8

Excessive bail shall not be required, nor excessive fines imposed, nor cruel and unusual punishments inflicted.

AMENDMENT 9

The enumeration in the Constitution of certain rights shall not be construed to deny or disparage others retained by the people.

AMENDMENT 10

The powers not delegated to the United States by the Constitution, nor prohibited by it to the States, are served to the States respectively, or to the people.

Text-Dependent Questions

1. What is the Constitution?
2. What is the Bill of Rights?
3. What type of cases does the U.S. Supreme Court hear?

Research Projects

1. Look up the history of the Bill of Rights. Why is this part of the Constitution? What rights and protections does it cover?

2. Investigate the decisions the Supreme Court has made this year. Which ones are most significant? Why?

3. Read the Second Amendment. The wording and punctuation are confusing to modern readers, resulting in endless debate about the extent of Americans' right to bear arms. Do some research on this topic. What is a "well-regulated militia?" What are "arms?" What do you think the writers of the amendment intended? As a practical matter, how should we interpret this amendment today?

CHAPTER 2

FEDERAL COURTS AND LAW ENFORCEMENT

Words to Understand

Cabinet: a body of advisers of a head of state

Duty: a tax on imports

Jurisdiction: an area, whether geographical or administrative, over which a court has authority

SOME LAWS ARE MADE BY THE STATE LEGISLATURES, OTHER LAWS ARE MADE BY CONGRESS. STATE, CITY AND COUNTY COURTS, AND LAW ENFORCEMENT AGENCIES ENFORCE STATE LAWS, WHILE FEDERAL LAWS ARE ENFORCED THROUGH THE FEDERAL COURTS, THE DEPARTMENT OF JUSTICE, AND VARIOUS SPECIALIZED ADMINISTRATIVE BODIES, SUCH AS THE INTERNAL REVENUE SERVICE (IRS), WHICH MAKES AND ENFORCES TAX LAWS. THE SUPREME COURT ALSO SETS UP RULES FOR THE FEDERAL COURT SYSTEM.

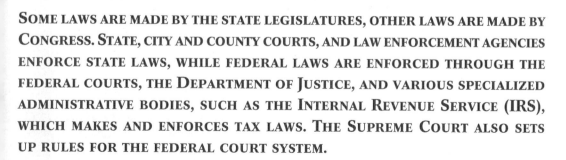

Coast Guard cutters, like this one near the Statue of Liberty in New York Harbor, patrol America's seashores. Since the tragedy of September 11, 2001, they have played a large role in protecting America's sea borders from terrorist attack.

The Federal Courts

The federal court system has **jurisdiction** over many different kinds of cases. They act as the trial court for some cases, the appeals court for others, and they also hear specialized cases, such as bankruptcy and tax cases. To manage this diverse workload, many different kinds of federal courts have been created over the years.

Some cases begin in the federal courts. They are heard in the federal district courts, which are trial courts. Those trial court decisions may be appealed to federal courts, called circuits. The country is divided into 13 circuits. Eleven circuits cover the states, each taking on between three and nine states. There is also a circuit court for Washington, D.C. The 13th circuit court, the Court of Appeals for the Federal Circuit, hears appeals of cases from specialized federal courts, such as the Patent and Trademark Office, the Court of Federal Claims, and the Court of International Trade. The 13 circuit courts of appeals hear appeals from the federal district courts as well as from federal administrative agencies and the bankruptcy courts. Decisions of the federal appellate courts can be appealed to the Supreme Court of the United States, if the Supreme Court grants an appeal. If a case is of national importance, and there is a conflict in the result between the circuits, the United States Supreme Court is likely to grant an appeal.

The Department of Justice

The Department of Justice (DOJ) has been called the largest law firm in the country. Instead of advising private clients, it gives advice to the federal government and also represents the government in the courts. Another function of the department is to enforce federal laws. It does this through such law enforcement agencies as the Federal Bureau of Investigation (FBI), the Drug Enforcement Administration (DEA), and the Immigration and Naturalization Service (INS).

The Attorney General is the head of the department. He or she is appointed by the president and sits on the president's **Cabinet**. In addition to running the department, the Attorney General gives advice to the president about legal matters.

Although there has been an Attorney General since 1789, when George Washington's own lawyer, Edmund Randolph, became the first Attorney General, the Department of Justice was not set up until 1870. In the early days of the United States, the Attorney General needed only to work part-time. Later, it became a full-time job, and as the country grew larger and more cases were

Copyright 1876 by Currier & Ives, N.Y.

GEORGE WASHINGTON. GEN: HENRY KNOX, Secy of War. ALEXANDER HAMILTON, Secy of the Treasury. THOMAS JEFFERSON, Secy of State. EDMUND RANDOLPH, Attorney General.

WASHINGTON AND HIS CABINET.

NEW YORK, PUBLISHED BY CURRIER & IVES, 125 NASSAU ST.

An illustration showing George Washington with his cabinet, Henry Knox, Alexander Hamilton, Thomas Jefferson, and Edmund Randolph.

heard, the Attorney General needed an assistant to handle the work. After the Civil War, there were many cases against the federal government; therefore, in 1870, Congress implemented an act creating the Department of Justice. It now has over 100,000 employees around the United States and a large annual budget, $21 billion in 2015.

The Solicitor General supervises the representation of the federal government before the Supreme Court and the federal appellate courts. Lawyers in the Solicitor General's department represent the government in these cases. Other federal court cases are handled by U.S. Attorneys. There are 95 U.S. Attorneys, with at least one assigned to every state. Large states have more than one. Each U.S. Attorney has a large staff of other attorneys who help with the work.

Jurisdiction

Federal courts have the power to decide only certain types of cases. This is called limited jurisdiction. They can hear only the kinds of cases specified in the Constitution or that Congress has given them power to hear under federal law. Under the Constitution, they have jurisdiction over questions involving the Constitution or treaties of the United States, cases involving ambassadors and certain other diplomats, and sea law. They rule on cases between states, between a state and a citizen of another state, between citizens of different states where the amount in dispute is over $75,000, and between U.S. states or citizens and foreign governments. Congress has also given the federal courts jurisdiction over a number of specialized areas, including international trade, bankruptcy, patents, trademarks, and tax.

The work in the Department of Justice is divided between six divisions: the Antitrust Division, the Civil Division, the Civil Rights Division, the Criminal Division, the Environment and Natural Resources Division, and the Tax Division. Each division employs lawyers to fight cases in their own area.

The Bureaus

In addition to being a law firm, the Department of Justice is also a law enforcement agency. Its role is to enforce federal law in both civil and criminal matters. The largest part of the Department of Justice is the Federal Bureau of Investigation (FBI). The FBI investigates violations of federal law. It also investigates cases in which the federal government is a party, and conducts other investigations on behalf of the government.

The Bureau of Prisons is in charge of federal prisons and is also dedicated to improving the welfare of prison inmates by providing them with jobs and training programs while they are in prison.

The Bureau of Alcohol, Tobacco, and Firearms (BATF) controls firearms and explosives. It also supervises the production, taxation, and distribution of alcohol and tobacco.

The U.S. Marshals have many responsibilities. They provide security in the federal courts, apprehend federal fugitives, operate the Federal Witness Protection program, transport federal prisoners, execute court orders and arrest warrants, and sell property forfeited in federal criminal cases, such as goods belonging to drug dealers.

Until 2003, the Immigration and Naturalization Service (INS) was in charge of immigration and applications for citizenship. Immigration is currently handled by U.S. Citizenship and Immigration Services (USCIS), which is part of the Department of Homeland Security, not the DOJ.

Immigrants are sworn in as citizens of the United States.

The Drug Enforcement Administration (DEA) leads the fight against drug trafficking. It enforces U.S. law in this area, presents criminal and civil cases, and acts internationally to stop drug production. The DEA works with the Coast Guard, Customs, and the Internal Revenue Service to stop high-level narcotics smuggling. The DEA also seizes the assets (goods and property) of drug traffickers.

Other Federal Law Enforcement Agencies

The Internal Revenue Service (IRS) administers and enforces tax laws.

United States Customs and Border Protection, which is part of the Department of Homeland Security, controls the entry of goods into the United States. The Customs Service collects taxes and **duties** on imports, and works to eliminate drug trafficking, as well as fighting customs fraud.

The United States Coast Guard assists in these efforts by patrolling the nation's sea borders and waterways. The Coast Guard is a part of the Department of Transportation, except in times of war, when it passes into the control of the Navy. The Coast Guard is responsible for keeping the waterways safe and for search-and-rescue operations. The Coast Guard has played a large role in patrolling the New England, New York, and New Jersey shores after the tragedy of September 11, 2001.

The Postal Inspection Service is the law enforcement arm of the U.S. Postal Service. It handles crimes that involve the mail, such as mail fraud and theft, child pornography, and mail bombs.

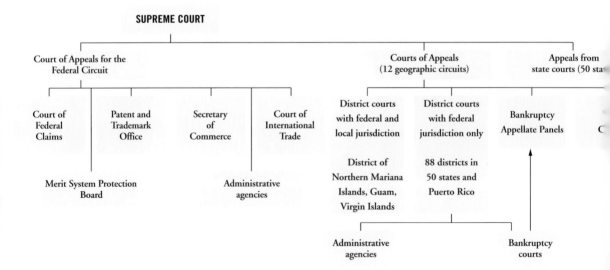

Text-Dependent Questions

1. What do the federal courts do?
2. What is the Department of Justice?
3. What is jurisdiction?

Research Projects

1. Investigate the many divisions of the Department of Justice. Where would you most like to work?
2. What do the U.S. Marshals do? What have been some of their more exciting cases?
3. The Drug Enforcement Agency handles drug trafficking. What sort of activities is the DEA currently engaged in?

THE FEDERAL BUREAU OF INVESTIGATION

Words to Understand

Fugitive: a person who is hiding from or running away from arrest

Latent: present and capable of becoming obvious, or active, even though not currently visible

Subversive: a person who systematically attempts to overthrow or undermine a government or political system by working secretly from within

ATTORNEY GENERAL CHARLES J. BONAPARTE SET UP THE FEDERAL BUREAU OF INVESTIGATION (FBI) AS A DIVISION OF THE DEPARTMENT OF JUSTICE IN 1908. FROM A SMALL GROUP OF 34 SPECIAL AGENTS, IT HAS BECOME ONE OF THE LARGEST AND MOST POWERFUL CRIME-FIGHTING AND INTELLIGENCE-GATHERING OPERATIONS IN THE WORLD, WITH AN ANNUAL BUDGET OF $3.57 BILLION (FISCAL YEAR 2001).

All FBI agents must undergo an intensive 16-week training at the FBI Academy in Quantico, Virginia, when they join the Bureau. In this class, they are learning how to defend themselves from an armed attack.

One of 32 federal agencies with law enforcement responsibilities, the FBI is the principal investigative arm of the Department of Justice; it is not a national police force. The FBI investigates crimes that are against federal law unless Congress has specifically assigned that type of crime to another government agency. For example, although tampering with the mail is against federal law, Congress has given the job of protecting the mail to the U.S. Postal Service.

The Priorities of the FBI

The FBI's main priority is the country's national and economic security. It investigates counterterrorism, foreign counterintelligence, and financial crime. It gathers data about people and organizations, both inside the United States and abroad, that it believes are potential threats to the country. Its second priority is criminal and public integrity, so it investigates organized crime and drugs, as well as civil rights violations. The Bureau's third priority is crimes against both individuals and property, so it targets violent crimes and major offenders.

The FBI has special responsibility for fighting terrorism.

The CIA

Established in 1947, the Central Intelligence Agency (CIA) protects the security of the United States from foreign threats. It works in secrecy, investigating foreign governments and their citizens who might harm the United States. The CIA also gathers intelligence on foreign drug-trafficking. It is not allowed to investigate or monitor anyone who is a U.S. citizen, resident alien, legal immigrant, or a U.S. corporation, whether it is based in the U.S. or abroad. Unlike the FBI, the CIA is not part of the U.S. Department of Justice, and it has no law enforcement powers.

The FBI gathers and reports facts, finds witnesses, and puts together evidence in cases that fall under the jurisdiction of federal law or that involve the federal government. The FBI also conducts background checks on people who apply for certain federal jobs, such as working in the White House. The FBI's headquarters are in Washington, D.C. The Bureau employs more than 35,000 people, including special agents and other employees. About one-third of its staff work in Washington, D.C., while the rest work around the country and the world. The FBI has 56 field offices, 400 satellite offices, and four special field units in the United States, as well as 40 foreign liaison posts.

Once the FBI has completed an investigation, it presents its findings to federal prosecutors, either at the Department of Justice or in the U.S. Attorney's Office. The prosecutors then decide if anyone will be prosecuted and how that case will be conducted.

The FBI has a special responsibility for crimes in which criminals move across state borders. They can help local and state police forces solve these crimes because they have the advantage of being able to access information from all over the country. Although the FBI works on crimes with state and local police forces, they do not take over the investigation and they are not in charge of the other police forces.

Wanted

The "Ten Most Wanted" posters were first distributed in 1950. At first, they were put up in post offices and police station to alert people to dangerous **fugitives** and criminals who were wanted by the FBI. Later, the FBI asked for the public's help on television. Over the years, many criminals have been brought to justice when people told FBI agents where they were. Two wanted criminals were even recognized when people touring the FBI building in Washington, D.C. spotted their photographs. Because these criminals are accused of violent crimes, the FBI urges the public not to approach them, as they may be armed and dangerous.

FBI TEN MOST WANTED FUGITIVE

Unlawful Flight to Avoid Prosecution - Criminal Homicide, Criminal Attempt to Commit Homicide in the First Degree, Criminal Homicide of a Law Enforcement Officer, Criminal Attempt to Commit Criminal Homicide of a Law Enforcement Officer

ERIC MATTHEW FREIN

Photograph taken in August of 2011

Aliases: Eric Frein, Eric M. Frein

DESCRIPTION

Date(s) of Birth Used:	May 3, 1983	**Hair:**	Brown
Place of Birth:	New Jersey	**Eyes:**	Blue
Height:	6'1"	**Sex:**	Male
Weight:	165 pounds	**Race:**	White
NCIC:	W011862497	**Nationality:**	American

Remarks: Frein is known to be a heavy smoker, a weapons enthusiast, and a survivalist. He claims to have fought with Serbians in Africa, and he has studied Russian and Serbian languages. He may have shaved his head on both sides and have long hair on top. He was last seen with no facial hair and was wearing a brown and gold windbreaker, khaki shorts, and sneakers. He was carrying a dark green backpack with black trim. Frein has ties to the mid-Atlantic region of the United States, including the states of Pennsylvania, New Jersey, and New York.

CAUTION

Eric Matthew Frein is wanted for his alleged involvement in the shooting death of one Pennsylvania State Police trooper and the wounding of another outside the Blooming Grove Barracks in Pike County, Pennsylvania, on September 12, 2014

REWARD

The FBI is offering a reward of up to $100,000 for information leading directly to the arrest of Eric Matthew Frein.

SHOULD BE CONSIDERED ARMED AND EXTREMELY DANGEROUS

If you have any information concerning this person, please contact your local FBI office or the nearest American Embassy or Consulate.

The FBI can help track down anyone who is on the run from the law. Called fugitives, these people might have escaped from a jail or courthouse or might be wanted by the police. If the fugitive crosses state lines or leaves the country, the FBI can issue a federal arrest warrant. At any one time, the FBI is searching for about 12,000 fugitives.

The fugitive's name and any identifying data are put into the National Crime Information Center's computer. Police and law enforcement officials all over the country can check the information there 24 hours a day, 365 days a year. It takes about two seconds to get a reply, and the computer handles 2.3 million transactions every day.

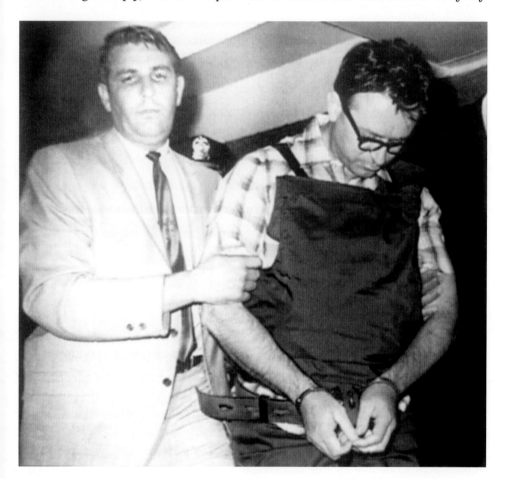

A **latent** fingerprint was found on the rifle that killed civil rights leader Dr. Martin Luther King, Jr. A search through FBI files revealed that it belonged to James Earl Ray. Ray was then arrested, tried, and found guilty of the murder.

The Identification System

The FBI keeps a national database of fingerprints and other forms of identification. In 2014 it introduced the Next Generation Identification (NGI) system, which improves on the former Integrated Automated Fingerprint Identification System (IAFIS). This system, started in 1999, contains fingerprints, criminal histories, photos of faces and tattoos, and physical characteristics of millions of criminals and criminal suspects, as well as fingerprints from millions of civilians. Police forces from around the country send in fingerprints they find at crime scenes or from suspects. If any of these match those of the fugitive, the police force that is looking for that person is notified. The system can generally match a fingerprint in less than 30 minutes. In one famous case, a latent fingerprint was found on the rifle used to kill Dr. Martin Luther King, Jr. The FBI matched it to a fingerprint from James Earl Ray, which led to his arrest and conviction for the murder of Dr. King.

Police departments across the country, and even around the world, receive help with their work. For example, the FBI began its Uniform Crime Report Program in 1929. This program receives, stores, and organizes data regarding serious crimes, such as murder, rape, robbery, and arson, from over 18,000 law enforcement agencies.

Other law enforcement agencies receive help from the FBI, who teach advanced crime-fighting techniques. State and local police can attend the FBI's national academy in Quantico, Virginia, or FBI agents can provide training locally through the Field Police Training Program.

The FBI runs the largest crime laboratory in the world. It examines evidence, not only for its own cases, but also provides this service free of charge for other law enforcement agencies. With the agreement of the Attorney General and the Secretary of State, it sometimes helps foreign police forces. At the FBI's laboratory, technicians analyze evidence, including blood, hair, fibers, glass, paint chips, and bullet wounds.

However, in the years following World War II, Hoover let his personal obsession with fighting Communism compromise the FBI. He set up investigations and kept files on people he suspected of being subversive, often using illegal methods, such as unauthorized wiretaps on their phones. He used dirty tricks and the threat of blackmail to silence anyone who might question him or the Bureau. After his death, the role of the FBI was reassessed. In 1975, the Church Committee, led by Senator Frank Church (D-Idaho), investigated the FBI's behavior and ordered it to focus on solving crimes.

John Dillinger

John Dillinger committed a string of bank robberies and daring escapes from prison in 1933 and 1934. In one prison escape, he carved a gun from a piece of wood, then painted it black with shoe polish and used the fake gun to intimidate the guards into letting him out. The sharply dressed Dillinger was wanted by the FBI because he and his gang robbed banks in several different states. Finally, the FBI got a tip and tracked him to the Biograph Movie Theater in Chicago, where they shot him dead.

J. Edgar Hoover

J. Edgar Hoover was the director of the FBI from 1924 to 1972. During his long career, he made the Bureau the top professional crime-fighting organization in the world, but also harmed its reputation by using illegal methods to investigate alleged **subversives**.

When Hoover became director, the Bureau of Investigation, as it was then known, was small and powerless. Over the next 10 years, however, Hoover changed that. He created a trained, professional crime-fighting force and set up a crime lab where evidence could be analyzed. Hoover and his Special Agents, or G-men, captured gangsters and bank robbers like John Dillinger. Hoover became famous for fighting crime.

Kidnappings and Missing Persons

The FBI also keeps a missing persons file. This is a database of runaways and other people whose families do not know where they are. As of 2014, there were more than 84,000 active missing person files. In 2013, 627,911 missing person records were entered into the system, but more than 630 records were removed over the same period, as law enforcement agencies located the people reported missing. At the FBI, computer technology is used to create a picture showing how a missing person might look now from a photograph taken before he or she disappeared, which can be many years previously in some cases. These photographs have successfully reunited many people with their families. If someone is kidnapped and taken across state lines, or if a young child is kidnapped, the FBI steps in. The FBI monitors all other kidnappings and offers help to the local or state police handling the case.

The FBI Critical Incidence Response Group helps other law enforcement agencies in times of crisis. This group has special training in the abduction and disappearance of children, crisis management, hostage negotiation, special weapons and tactics, and criminal investigative analysis.

Certain kinds of bombings also come under the jurisdiction of the FBI. If a terrorist or a revolutionary group is suspected of having planted a bomb, if a bombing occurs on a college or university campus, or if a bombing is carried out against a U.S. citizen or institution abroad, then the FBI is responsible for investigating it.

Guarding Civil Rights

The FBI is also charged with making sure that people can enjoy their civil rights, no matter what gender, race, color, religion, or nationality they are. As part of this responsibility, they investigate hate groups, who threaten to use force to get their way, and could carry out that threat, possibly breaking federal law.

There are also FBI task forces that concentrate on organized crime, bank robbery, kidnapping, terrorism, and motor vehicle theft. These task forces allow the FBI and local and state police to work together and to share information about these serious crimes.

Text-Dependent Questions

1. What is the FBI?
2. What are some of the files and databases the FBI maintains?
3. What is the FBI's civil rights role?

Research Projects

1. Look up the FBI's Next Generation Identification System. What capabilities does it have? What areas is the FBI planning to upgrade and improve as technology becomes available?
2. Investigate the history of the FBI. Who was J.Edgar Hoover? How did his particular interests influence the FBI's work? How has the Bureau changed in recent years?
3. How does the FBI go about locating missing persons? How many missing persons remain unfound forever?

CHAPTER 4

THE POLICE

Words to Understand

Deputy: a person appointed as a substitute with power to act

Felony: the most serious category of crime, carrying a penalty of more than one year in jail

Misdemeanor: a lesser crime, punishable by less than one year in jail

Ordinance: a law set forth by a governmental authority

IN THE UNITED STATES, OVER 40,000 LOCAL, COUNTY, AND STATE POLICE DEPARTMENTS ENFORCE THE LAW. ALL OF THESE DIFFERENT AGENCIES USE DIFFERENT PROCEDURES AND REPORT TO DIFFERENT GOVERNMENT BODIES. SOME REPORT TO THE STATE GOVERNOR, OTHERS TO THE CITY COUNCIL OR MAYOR, AND STILL OTHERS DIRECTLY TO THE VOTERS. ALL OF THEM, AS THEY GO ABOUT THE BUSINESS OF KEEPING THE PEACE, HOWEVER, MUST RESPECT THE ULTIMATE LAW OF THE UNITED STATES: THE CONSTITUTION.

Enforcing the Law

With all these different agencies, and the more than one million officers who serve in them, trying to enforce the law, there ought to be a lot of confusion, but there is not. Each law enforcement body has jurisdiction over a particular area, perhaps a city or town, as in the case of a local police department; perhaps the

Here, a local police officer takes a "mug shot" before fingerprinting a potential suspect in a felony. Much of modern police work is administrative, with officers having to make out crime reports and interview witnesses as part of the crime investigation.

highway, as with the state police; or perhaps the courts and unincorporated parts of the county, as with county sheriffs. When their jurisdictions overlap, such as when a speeding motorist drives down the highway into another town or state, the different law enforcement agencies work together to catch the offender. This can occasionally lead to confusion as to whose jurisdiction a particular offense is in, but generally the system works well.

All the different law enforcement agencies in the country have the same mission: to protect and serve. They take crime reports, investigate crimes, interview witnesses, collect evidence, arrest people suspected of crimes, and later testify against them at their trials.

The Local Police, Sheriffs, and State Police

Police officers are employed by the local authority, no matter what size the police department may be. In a big city, they are under the supervision of a police commission. In a small town, they are supervised directly by the city council, mayor, or city manager, depending on the structure of the local government. As well as enforcing federal and state laws, local police officers also enforce city or town **ordinances**. In most places, however, they do not enforce zoning regulations or ordinances. As well as investigating crimes and making arrests, the police keep order, direct traffic, help people, find lost children, and give assistance in an emergency.

The head of county police departments are sheriffs, who are often elected to this position. Their two main jobs are helping to run the county courthouse, including the county jail, and enforcing the law in parts of the county that do not come under the jurisdiction of any local police department. The sheriff and his or her **deputies** can also help local police departments if they are asked to. Some states do not have county police.

The Texas Rangers, established in 1835, were the first statewide law enforcement agency. Now, every state has a state police department. The state police report directly to the governor. They have jurisdiction over the highways and crimes that occur in more than one town, as well as tracing stolen cars. They also help with crowd control and public disturbances.

Law Enforcement and the Constitution

The Bill of Rights tells the police how they must act when they are arresting someone or collecting evidence. Because the Constitution is more powerful than any person or organization in the country, the police must obey it. It is up to the

Here, county police in California apprehend a man suspected of drug dealing. County sheriffs and their deputies are often elected by their local constituents.

courts to decide whether or not the police have acted legally in specific cases.

The men who wrote the Constitution and the Bill of Rights gave the individual plenty of rights because under British rule, officials had often searched people's houses and arrested them, either to harass them or because of their political beliefs. The Bill of Rights made sure that this could never happen in the United States.

The Fourth Amendment gives general advice about the state's right to search and seize people and their property. It reads: "The right of the people to be secure in their persons, houses, papers, and effects, against unreasonable searches and seizures shall not be violated, and no Warrants shall issue but upon probable cause, supported by Oath or affirmation, and particularly describing the place to be searched, and the persons or things to be seized."

Radios allow police officers to keep in touch with each other, enabling them to call for backup if they need help or to radio ahead with a description of a suspect.

The police use specially trained dogs to find drugs and explosives. The dogs can smell such substances even when these are hidden in suitcases or inside cars.

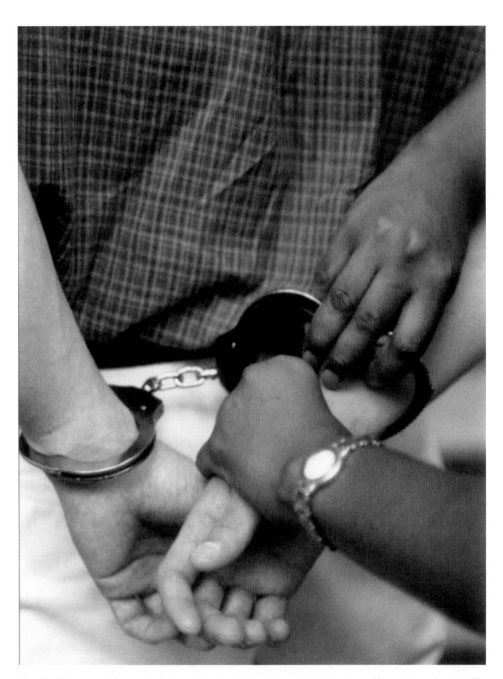

Handcuffs are used to control suspects who are under arrest. Here, an officer places handcuffs around a suspect's wrist. Sometimes, plastic handcuffs are used, or the suspect's hands might be cuffed together in front of him, instead of behind him.

Over the years, the Supreme Court has clarified and explained what this long, complicated sentence means. Basically, the police cannot arrest anyone or search their property unless they have a good reason (probable cause). To make a search or an arrest, they usually need to have written permission (a warrant), signed by a judge to whom they have explained why there is probable cause. This permission must state exactly who they are arresting, where they want to search, and what they are looking for. If the police do not follow the procedures correctly, then when the case comes to court, the judge might not allow the evidence they find to be presented, possibly allowing someone who is guilty to go free. In addition, the police department, or even the officer personally involved, might be sued by the person whose rights were violated. It is, therefore, essential that police officers understand and follow the rules.

Probable cause means that the facts, as viewed by a reasonable observer, point to a suspect's guilt. It does not mean that the person is definitely guilty; that is for a future trial in a court to decide.

Making an Arrest

The police have the right to stop someone for questioning. If the person is not free to leave, the stop becomes an arrest, even if the officer does not say, "You are under arrest." Usually, to arrest a suspect, the police need an arrest warrant that has been signed by a judge, but if the police actually see someone committing a crime, they can arrest that person without a warrant. Once the arrest has been made, they can also search the person and take photographs and fingerprints. They can also search the area immediately around the person without a warrant.

For example, the police can stop a car to question the driver if they see him or her driving oddly. If they smell marijuana in the car, they can search the car for drugs and arrest the person if they find them. They could also search the inside of the car and any bags or suitcases inside the car. If they wanted to search the car again later, however, they would need a warrant.

Usually, the police need a warrant to make an arrest or conduct a search. The application for the warrant must explain the reasons for the arrest or search. Searching an apartment because it is in an area where many people use drugs is not a good enough reason. There would be probable cause to search an apartment where something suspicious is going on, such as many different people going in with televisions and coming out carrying money, making a reasonable person believe that someone in the apartment was receiving stolen goods. The warrant would have to say exactly what the police are looking for. If the search warrant is for stolen televisions, the police cannot look in desk drawers because these are too small to conceal a television. But the police can look at and seize anything illegal that is out in the open. So, if they saw drugs in plain view on the kitchen table, they could seize them and make an arrest.

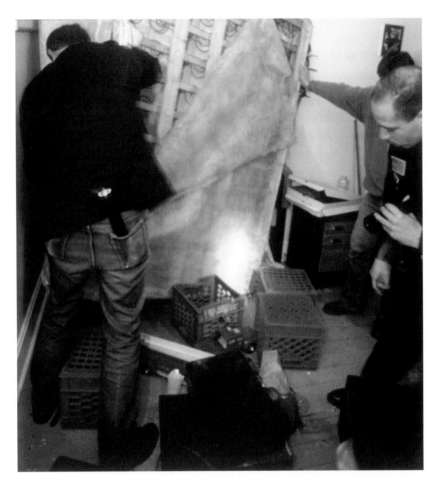

These police officers are searching an apartment for drugs. Because the packages containing drugs are often very small, the police have the right to search even the smallest spaces in order to look for them.

The Miranda Warning

In the case of Ernesto Miranda, the Supreme Court ruled in 1966 that the police had to let a suspect know what his rights were under the Constitution before questioning him. Ernesto Miranda had confessed to rape and kidnapping without being informed of his rights. The Supreme Court, therefore, ruled that his confession could not be used against him at a trial. A typical Miranda warning reads: "You have a right to remain silent, anything you say can and will be used against you in a court of law. You have a right to have an attorney present; one will be appointed for you if you cannot afford one."

Once the police have made an arrest, they take the suspect to the station and book him or her for the crime. Later, in some **misdemeanors** and in all **felonies**, a prosecutor or a grand jury will decide if there is enough evidence for the person to be charged with the crime and for the case to go to trial. If there is not enough evidence, the suspect will be released, but might be arrested again later if more evidence is found.

Some people think that the rules of arrest and search and seizure make it too easy for the suspect to be found not guilty on a technicality and too hard for the police to catch criminals. But because the police have so much power and the individual has so little, the protection that the Bill of Rights gives us is very important. The great Supreme Court justice and legal thinker Oliver Wendell Holmes said, "It is a less evil that some criminals should escape than that the government should play an ignoble part."

Text-Dependent Questions

1. What do police do?
2. How does the Bill of Rights limit what law enforcement officers can do?
3. What is a warrant?

Research Projects

1. What is the Fourth Amendment? How does that affect the work of law enforcement?
2. Investigate law enforcement in your state. What agency handles matters at the city level? Who takes care of the county? What are your state police called? Are there other law enforcement agencies? What do they do? How do all these agencies work together?
3. What is the Miranda warning? Why is it important?

CHAPTER 5

THE COURTS

Words to Understand

Acquittal: a setting free from the charge of an offense by verdict, sentence, or other legal process

Bail: amount of money pledged to the court as a promise that the accused will appear at trial

Compensation: an appropriate and usually counterbalancing payment

Embezzlement: to appropriate fraudulently for one's own use

Probation: period of supervision outside prison, usually accompanied by certain rules. If these are violated, a prison sentence is imposed

Statute: a law enacted by the legislative branch of a government

Subpoena: to serve someone with a writ, commanding the person designated in it to appear in court under a penalty for failure

Waive: to relinquish voluntarily

THE U.S. COURT SYSTEM IS LARGE AND COMPLEX. IT INCLUDES EVERY COURT, FROM THE SMALLEST TRAFFIC COURT, TO THE HIGHEST COURT IN THE LAND, THE SUPREME COURT, WHERE ISSUES THAT AFFECT THE LIVES OF MANY MILLIONS OF AMERICANS ARE DECIDED.

In the United States, there are six sources of law. The first is the Constitution, including the Bill of Rights. Statutory law is made by our elected representatives at both the state and the federal level. Administrative law covers rules for filing

The American democratic system of government—represented by the scales of justice—depends on a fair and independent court system.

your tax return. Common law, which comes from 12th-century England, forms the basis of the law of the United States and most other English-speaking countries. Case law comes from decisions made in earlier cases, some of which might have been decided over 100 years ago. Judges use all these different types of law to decide cases in court.

Civil vs. Criminal Cases

Two different types of cases come before the courts: civil cases and criminal cases. In civil cases, one person sues another in a dispute over money or property. Most of these cases are about such things as contracts, whose fault an accident was, whether a will was legal or not, or family problems, such as divorce or child custody and support. The person who brings the lawsuit is called the plaintiff and the one who is sued is called the defendant. Most of the cases tried in the United States are civil cases.

In criminal cases, the, court has to decide if a person accused of a crime is guilty or not. Criminal cases are not argued between the victim and the accused, but between the state and the accused. This is because crimes are considered to be offenses against society as a whole, not just against the person who is the victim. Criminal offenses include murder, theft, assault, **embezzlement**, abuse, and arson.

Although court procedures in civil and criminal cases have much in common, there are many important differences. Most important, in criminal cases, the accused, known in court as the defendant, has to be proven guilty beyond a reasonable doubt. This standard of proof is higher than in a civil case, where proof is based on the preponderance of evidence—that is, based on the evidence presented in court, the defendant is judged more likely than not to have engaged in the acts or behavior claimed by the plaintiff. The criminal standard of proof is higher, because being found guilty of a crime carries much worse penalties than losing a civil case does. If a criminal defendant is found guilty, he or she can be imprisoned, thus losing his or her freedom. In some criminal cases, for example, murder or treason, the defendant can even be executed if found guilty.

The Federal Courts

The court system in the United States is multitiered. Cases begin in the lower courts and can then be appealed to the upper courts. There are two parallel court systems: the federal courts and the state courts. The federal courts have jurisdiction over certain civil and criminal cases. They can hear cases about federal crimes, federal constitutional law, cases involving the residents of two different states, disputes between U.S. citizens and citizens of foreign countries, and cases that involve both federal **statutes** and sometimes state statutes. The highest court in the federal system is the U.S. Supreme Court.

The State Courts

The state courts have jurisdiction over all the other cases in the United States. Every state has its own court system. The courts even have different names: what one state calls a city court, another might call a municipal court, Justice of the Peace court, county, or circuit court. Some courts decide only certain kinds of cases, such as traffic violations or minor criminal cases. These are called limited jurisdiction courts, and the cases that they can hear are set out in the state constitution or by the state legislature. In general, these courts hear civil cases that involve small amounts of money (usually less than $2,000) and criminal cases where the penalty is less than one year in jail.

Higher trial courts, known as general jurisdiction courts, hear more serious criminal cases and civil cases in which a large amount of money is in dispute. Different states have different cutoff points for when a case should move to the higher court and different names for these courts, including circuit court, superior court, district court, and court of common

A federal court judge takes notes during a difficult murder trial. Courtrooms today are very high-tech, and court officials are able to access important material relating to a case via an internal computer network.

pleas. Most states divide their court system into districts based on geographical areas so that people do not have to travel too far to go to court. All of these different courts are trial courts, and despite their differences, the procedures they use to try cases are similar.

Furthermore, different states define criminal offenses in different ways and award different penalties for these offenses. A murder in Connecticut could result in the death penalty; murder in Rhode Island, a neighboring state, can result only in a maximum sentence of life imprisonment.

The Supreme Court in Washington, D.C., is the court of last resort. It is the last place to appeal a lower-court decision. The Court decides which cases to listen to and hears only appeals that are of national importance.

This county courtroom is typical of thousands across the United States. At the front is the bench where the judge sits. To the right is the witness box. The court officials and lawyers for the defense and the prosecution sit at tables in front of the judge.

The Appellate Courts

The next level above the trial courts are the appellate courts. As their name suggests, these courts listen to appeals. In a civil case, either the plaintiff or the defendant can appeal if he or she loses, but in a criminal case, usually only the accused, known as the defendant, can appeal. This is because the Bill of Rights outlaws double jeopardy, guaranteeing that a person can only be tried once for the same offense. If the state was allowed to appeal after the accused had been found not guilty, it would violate the double jeopardy rule, since it would be a second trial for the same offense. However, it has been known for a defendant to be tried on a different aspect of an earlier offense.

An appeal is based on a point of law that the trial judge decided incorrectly or on an abuse of the trial court's discretion. The appellate court does not hold a new trial. Instead, the court reviews the decision and procedures of the lower court. On appeal, the attorneys for both sides would usually be present. They present legal arguments about the decision and procedures of the lower court. No new evidence is presented. At the end of the hearing, the judge can either say that the trial court was right, known as upholding the decision of the lower court, or say that it was wrong, known as reversing the decision. The appeal court can, in some cases, modify the amount of the award in a civil trial. A reversal usually requires a new trial.

State supreme courts are the highest courts in the state system. Most states have only one supreme court, but Oklahoma and Texas have two: one to hear civil cases, the other to hear criminal cases. Some cases are heard by the U.S. Supreme Court after being heard in the state supreme court if the U.S. Supreme Court grants a petition allowing the case to be heard.

Witch Trials

Centuries ago, people were often tried by ordeal rather than by evidence presented against them. For example, a woman accused of witchcraft would be thrown into deep water. If she floated, the judges believed that she had used magic to save herself and was therefore guilty. If she sank, she was innocent. Few people survived this type of trial—those who proved their innocence by sinking, usually drowned before they could be rescued. Those who did not drown were judged to be guilty and subsequently burned at the stake.

The Judicial Selection Process

The methods for selecting judges vary. In federal courts, judges are nominated, usually by senators or the president. In state courts, judges are elected or appointed. Appointments are usually made by the governor, then approved by the state's senate or house of representatives.

Judges serve for long terms, sometimes for life. They are removed from the federal bench for only three reasons: committing an illegal act, abusing their power, or being incompetent or senile. The reasons for removing a state judge are similar.

The Adversary System

Once the case comes to trial, lawyers speak for the parties in court, although people have the right to represent themselves if they want to do so. In most criminal cases, the defendant has a right to a lawyer, and the court will appoint one if the defendant cannot afford one.

The United States has an adversarial system. This means that both sides get the same chance to explain their case and to attack the case of the other side. Cases are heard before a judge, who acts like a sort of umpire, making sure that things are fair for both sides and that everyone is doing things according to the rules. The judge has to remain impartial and neutral.

During a trial, the judge remains neutral, responsible for ensuring that the court gives both sides a fair hearing. A judge often allows lawyers for the defense and the prosecution to take a few minutes to confer with other members of their legal teams.

This man is being sworn in as a witness. He promises that the testimony he is about to give is the truth, the whole truth, and nothing but the truth. Lying on the witness stand, or perjury, is a serious crime that carries severe penalties, including jail.

What Happens at a Criminal Trial

Criminal cases are tried in the trial courts, either in courts of limited jurisdiction or in courts of general jurisdiction, depending on the severity of the offense. All courts try cases according to the same general principles, although the specific procedures vary from state to state. The judge presides over the trial. The judge decides points of law and makes sure both sides present their cases in an orderly way and according to the rules. Under the Constitution, everyone accused of a crime has a right to trial by jury. In a jury trial, the judge decides legal issues, but the jury decides whether or not the accused is guilty.

Sometimes the defendant **waives** the right to a jury trial, and the judge alone hears the case. This is called a bench trial. In some states, usually involving a charge of murder, a panel of three judges may hear the case.

The prosecution in a criminal case is the state, sometimes known as "the people." This is because a crime is an offense against the state, not against the victim of the crime. The victim appears in court as a witness for the prosecution and, in some states, has the right to speak at the sentencing of a defendant if the defendant is found guilty.

The Preliminary Hearings

Before the actual trial, there may be a number of hearings. At the first hearing, often called the preliminary hearing, or probable cause hearing, the judge makes sure that a crime has been committed and that the prosecution has enough evidence to show that the defendant probably committed the crime. If the judge feels there is not enough evidence, the accused has to be released, but he or she can be arrested again if more evidence is discovered later.

Hearsay

Testimony by a witness of what someone else said is called hearsay and is usually not admissible in court for the following reasons. Hearsay statements were not made under oath and so might not be true. Because the jury cannot see the speaker, they cannot determine whether or not he or she is telling the truth. In addition, the defendant has a right to question anyone who testifies against him and cannot do so if that person is not in the courtroom. One of the few cases in which hearsay is allowed is if it is a dying declaration. If someone knows she is dying and someone else hears her gasp, "John shot me!" her statement is admissible even though it is hearsay.

Next comes the indictment. At this hearing, the defendant is formally accused of the crime. In about half the states and in all federal cases, the accused is indicted by a grand jury. A grand jury is a panel of people picked at random who meet to decide if the accused should stand trial. They rarely decide not to indict. In states that do not use grand juries, the accused is indicted based on the state prosecutor's opinion that there is enough evidence, called the "information." Afterward, there is a **bail** hearing to find out if the accused has to stay in jail until it is time for the trial or not.

At the next hearing, called the arraignment, the judge notifies the accused of the charges and asks how he or she pleads. The accused may plead not guilty, *nolo contendere* (Latin for "I do not contest"), or guilty to the charges. There is a fourth type of plea called the "Alford" in which the defendant agrees the state has enough evidence to convict and will probably get a conviction, but the defendant does not admit guilt. It usually has the same consequences as a guilty plea.

Plea Bargaining

In criminal cases, the prosecution often agrees to lower the charge or to recommend a reduced sentence if the defendant pleads guilty. About 90 percent of all criminal cases do not go to trial because a deal is struck. This saves money and time (prosecutors usually have too much work), guarantees that the defendant is punished, and is attractive to the defendant because a conviction would mean a much longer prison term.

After any pleas—except not guilty—the next step is sentencing. If the crime is serious, the case is usually continued so that a presentencing investigation can be prepared by the **probation** department for the judge to use in determining the appropriate length of sentence. The report may also say if probation is an alternative to all or some of the sentence. Some states prescribe set terms of imprisonment, while others require mandatory minimums for some crimes, leaving the judge no discretion; and some states give the judge the power to sentence between a range of years.

A not guilty plea means there has to be a trial to find out if the accused is guilty or not. The two sides have a period of time in which to prepare their cases. During this period, there might be a pretrial conference so the two sides

After the case has been presented, the jury goes away to make its decision. First the members elect a foreman or forewoman to lead the discussions and present their verdict to the court. The forewoman of this jury is reading out their verdict.

can decide if there is anything that they can agree on. If they can agree on certain aspects of the case, time will not be wasted at the trial. Before the trial, both sides also file documents, called motions, with the court, stating what evidence they have and who their witnesses are. There are no surprise witnesses in real-life trials. The defendant might file motions to suppress evidence or to suppress a confession.

The law applies to everyone, even the richest people in the country. Here, Bill Gates, accompanied by his wife Melinda, arrives at the U.S. District Court in Washington, D.C. to testify in an anti-trust suit brought by the U.S. Department of Justice against his company, Microsoft in 2001.

The Trial

The first step at the trial is to pick the jury. All of the potential jurors are interviewed. Both the prosecution and the defense are allowed to accept or reject a certain number of jurors, according to certain rules. Each side wants to find jurors who will be fair, and hopefully even sympathetic, to its side.

When all the jurors have been selectd, the trial begins. At the trial, both sides present their evidence before the judge and jury. The state has to prove that the accused committed the crime; the accused does not have to prove that he or she did not do it. This is because the state has what is known as the burden of proof. Under the Constitution, a person is considered innocent until proven guilty.

The prosecution calls witnesses and produces evidence against the accused. During cross-examination, the defense can question the witnesses in order to show that their evidence is not valid.

The defense presents its case next. Witnesses and evidence are used to show that there are other explanations for what happened than the defendant's guilt. The prosecution has a chance to cross-examine the defense witnesses to try to expose any flaws in their testimony.

At the end of the trial in the closing statements, the prosecution explains the ways in which they have proved the defendant's guilt beyond a reasonable doubt to the jury. Then the defense points out any facts in the trial that could make a reasonable person doubt the guilt of the accused.

The judge then sums up the legal issues in the case for the jury. The judge tells the jury how the law applies to the case, but not what the verdict should be. The judge explains what reasonable doubt means, reminding the jury that there does not have to be absolute proof of guilt, only good reason to believe the defendant is guilty.

Civil vs. Criminal

There are different rules for hearing civil and criminal cases. This chart lets you see the differences at a glance.

Criminal	Civil
Who are the parties in the trial?	
Plaintiff: The state, represented by the prosecutor	Plaintiff: The victim of the wrongdoing
versus	
Defendant: The accused	Defendant: The person the victim accuses of doing something wrong
What is the standard of proof?	
Guilt beyond a reasonable doubt	Fault based on a preponderance of the evidence, or, in some cases, proof of clear and convincing evidence

What rights does the defendant have?

The right to remain silent

The right to have the case heard before a jury

The right to a jury trial

The right to a lawyer paid for by the state if he or she can't afford one

The right to a unanimous decision by the jury

The right to be tried only once for a crime

If the defendant is found guilty, what happens?	
The offender gets punished by a fine, community service or probation, or a prison term	The victim (plaintiff) gets financial compensation from the defendant

The jury makes their decision in private. They must all agree on the verdict. In most states the verdict in a criminal trial must be unanimous, but in some states, a 10/2 or an 11/1 verdict is allowed. If the jury cannot agree, there is a "hung jury," or a mistrial.

Juries can find the defendant not guilty, guilty as charged, or guilty of a lesser charge (such as manslaughter instead of murder). If the jury finds the defendant not guilty, he or she goes free and can never be tried for that crime again. If the jury finds the defendant guilty, the judge sentences the defendant to prison or some other punishment.

However, the case may not end, even after a guilty verdict. The defense lawyers will try to find places during the trial where the judge decided points of law incorrectly. If they can find something that the judge did wrong, they can appeal to a higher court to have the decision reversed, or to get a new trial If the appeals court determines that the evidence was not sufficient to find the defendant guilty, a judgment of **acquittal** must follow and the defendant must be released.

Some cases are appealed all the way to the Supreme Court because states cannot make laws that conflict with the U.S. Constitution. It is up to the Supreme Court to decide if a state law contradicts the Constitution. A state can, however, give defendants greater rights under the state's constitution than the federal constitution does.

Civil Cases

If two people have an argument and cannot agree on how to settle it, one of them might sue the other, asking the court to decide who is right. There are as many subjects for civil cases as there are things to argue about, but they usually fall into two categories: contracts (written or verbal agreements) and torts (wrongful acts).

In contract cases, one person believes that the other has broken, or breached, the contract (whether verbal or written) by not doing something that he was supposed to. For example, you agree to sell your friend a car and receive the money in installments, but he never pays the full amount. If he will not pay you and he will not give the car back, you might ask the court to make him stick to the agreement.

In torts cases, one person claims that the other has wronged him or her, either intentionally, as with assault, or negligently as the result of an accident or unforeseen consequence of his or her actions. For example, someone crashes into your car, wrecking it. You might ask the court to decide whose fault it was and how much that person should be required to pay to fix the damage.

In civil cases, both parties can agree not to have a jury trial. Then a judge alone may hear the case (a bench trial). Lawyers often prefer bench trials when the issues are technical, perhaps involving scientific questions, or if they think that the jury will become too emotionally involved in the case. Either side may choose a jury trial.

Here, Heyward Patterson, one of the nine young men accused of raping two white women in Scottsboro, Alabama, holds two talismans (a rabbit's foot and a horseshoe) during the court proceedings at his retrial in 1933.

Due Process of Law

On March 25, 1931, nine young black men were arrested for raping two white women in a railroad car in Scottsboro, Alabama. Two weeks after the arrest, the youths were found guilty and sentenced to death, except the youngest, aged 13, whose case ended in a mistrial. They appealed to the Alabama Supreme Court on the grounds that they had not been allowed proper legal representation, that the jury was all-white, and that the atmosphere in the town was so hostile that a fair trial was impossible. The court rejected the appeal.

Then the Supreme Court of the United States agreed to hear the appeal. The Supreme Court reversed the convictions on the grounds that the defendants had not been allowed legal representation. The 14th Amendment says that states must not "deprive anyone of life, liberty, or property, without due process of the law." The justices said that part of due process is the right to a fair trial. The Supreme Court found that without a lawyer, no defendant could get a fair trial because he or she could not effectively present his or her case. Not having a lawyer was, therefore, a denial of due process.

This landmark decision guaranteed poor defendants free legal representation in criminal trials. However, it did not immediately free the Scottsboro Boys—four of the men were not released until 1937, the other five either escaped or were paroled only after many years in prison.

O.J. Simpson

The "double jeopardy" rule prevents the state from trying someone twice for a crime, but often, one crime can result in two cases, one civil and the other criminal. Even if there is not enough evidence for a jury to find the accused guilty beyond a reasonable doubt in a criminal trial, there may be enough evidence to cause him to lose a civil case since the standard of proof is not as high. The plaintiff only has to prove that a wrong was committed based on the preponderance of the evidence. Also, in a criminal case, the defendant does not have to testify, while in a civil case he can be **subpoenaed** as a witness.

The best-known case of this kind concerns O.J. Simpson. He was found not guilty in October 1995 of the murders of his ex-wife Nicole Brown Simpson and a local waiter Ronald Goldman. However, he was found guilty of wrongful death in a civil case brought by the estates of the two murder victims and was ordered to pay $33.5 million in damages.

Before a civil trial begins, there is a pretrial process called discovery, in which the lawyers let each other know what evidence they will be producing in court. They might also agree that certain facts are true before the trial begins. This saves time and money at the trial. If one side sees that the other side's case is strong during discovery, they might decide to settle the case. This means coming to an agreement about the case before the trial. It often makes sense to settle civil cases out of court, because no one can know for sure how a judge or jury will decide. Both sides save legal fees by settling. The defense can negotiate what the accused has to pay, and the plaintiff can be sure of getting some **compensation**. If the case went to trial, the plaintiff might lose and not get anything at all, or the defendant might have to pay a lot more compensation.

If the case does go to trial, the plaintiff and the defendant call witnesses, present evidence, and make arguments in the same way as in a criminal case. At the end of the case, in a jury trial, the jury decides which side is in the right and awards damages against the defendant if the plaintiff wins. Sometimes, defendants are also ordered to pay punitive damages, an extra amount to punish them financially for their actions. It is up to the plaintiff, not the court, to collect the damages from the defendant, and this can sometimes be difficult.

In a civil case, either side can appeal the decision. As in a criminal case, a person appeals if he or she thinks that the judge has made an incorrect ruling about the law during the trial. The losing side can also appeal to have the amount of damages awarded reduced.

Text-Dependent Questions

1. What is the difference between civil and criminal cases?
2. What is the difference between federal and state courts?
3. What is an appeal?

Research Projects

1. How is your state's court system organized? What types of cases do the different courts hear?
2. Are your judges elected or appointed? Which do you think produces more fairness in court decisions?
3. Learn more about the process of a criminal trial. Why are there so many different steps and rules?

FAMILY COURTS AND THE JUVENILE JUSTICE SYSTEM

Words to Understand

Fine: to impose a monetary penalty on
Juvenile: young, not considered an adult, usually under the age of 18
Mental capacity: intelligence and understanding

THE NUMBER OF PEOPLE UNDER 18 WHO ARE ARRESTED HAS GONE DOWN IN RECENT YEARS. IN 2012, LAW ENFORCEMENT AGENCIES MADE 1.3 MILLION ARRESTS OF PEOPLE UNDER 18, 37 PERCENT LESS THAN IN 2003. TEENS AND YOUNGER CHILDREN ARE ARRESTED FOR THE FULL RANGE OF CRIME, INCLUDING MURDER, RAPE, AND VIOLENT ASSAULT, THOUGH THEFT IS THE MOST COMMON CAUSE OF ARREST.

Mothers Against Drunk Driving (MADD) is a pressure group set up by the mothers of young people killed by drunk drivers. They have succeeded in getting harsher penalties for drinking and driving and raising public awareness of the dangers of driving while intoxicated.

Family law, involving both divorce courts and the **juvenile** courts, is one that many children and teenagers might encounter in their lives. This is because half of all marriages end in divorce, and there are many single parent families dependent on child support. In addition, nearly three million young people are arrested each year in the United States.

Juvenile Justice

Many people believe that what you do when you are under 18 does not count later and that juvenile courts are easy on young people. They think that when someone under 18 commits an offense, it is always dealt with in the juvenile court system and that what happens there is kept private, both at the time and later on.

In fact, some children under 18 are tried in adult courts—and sent to adult prisons—if their offense is a serious one. In some states, journalists can attend juvenile court hearings and even publish the names of juveniles under certain circumstances; and in some states, juvenile records can be used to help decide sentencing if the offender is later convicted as an adult.

Juvenile courts hear cases involving underage children (known legally as minors) who live with and are supported by their parents. Children are minors until they are 16 in some states, but until they are 19 in Wyoming. In addition to cases of criminal conduct, the juvenile courts also hear cases of abuse or neglect and status cases. Status offenses are things like skipping school (truancy), which is only an offense if you are underage.

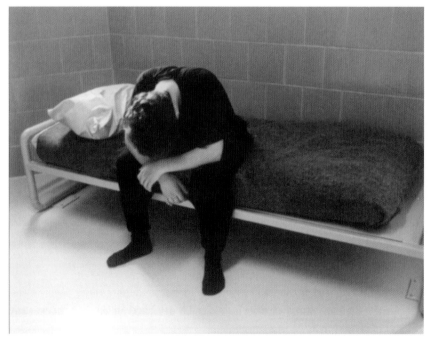

Being locked up in a cell, like this one at a juvenile detention facility, is a frightening experience for many young people. Young people have the same legal rights as adults, including the right to a lawyer and the right to remain silent.

Graffiti was once considered a minor offense; the police might simply have reprimanded those involved and made them clean the wall. Now, partly because graffiti has become so widespread, putting graffiti on walls will probably lead to being taken into custody and charged.

Children younger than eight or nine do not have the **mental capacity** to commit a crime. In other words, they do not necessarily have the ability at this age to tell the difference between right and wrong. So, even if they do something wrong, it is not a criminal offense. When a very young child hurts or even kills someone, for example, while playing with a gun, it is regarded as an accident, not as a crime, because the child is believed to be too young to understand the consequences of his or her actions. Children over the age of eight or nine, however, are old enough to understand that if you shoot someone, you might hurt or even kill that person, so they can be charged with a crime.

In some states, juveniles (sometimes as young as 13, depending on the state) can be tried as adults. This usually applies to older children and to more serious crimes. Some states have passed laws transferring the cases of minors accused of certain crimes to adult courts. At other times, the juvenile court judge can decide at a transfer hearing that a minor should be tried as an adult.

New Jersey V.T.L.O.

In this case, a student's purse was searched after she was caught smoking cigarettes with a friend, and marijuana was found. The girl (known by the initials T.L.O.) sued the school for unreasonable search and seizure. She said that under the Fourth Amendment the school had no right to search her purse without probable cause. The school argued that they were acting in *loco parentis*, Latin for "in place of the parent," rather than as a government agency. Therefore, they did not need permission to search her property while she was at school. The court decided that students had only a limited right to privacy because that right had to be balanced against the school's duty to maintain discipline and to keep students safe while they were at school.

This police officer is patrolling a housing project. As he goes by, he talks to local residents, including children like this girl. To fight crime effectively, the police need to make sure that local people know and trust them.

In adult courts, minors are treated as adults and face all the same rules, including those regarding sentencing. If convicted, they are sent to adult prisons. If they were over 16 at the time of committing the crime, they can even get the death penalty.

The Arrest

In general, minors have the same rights as an adult. The police cannot search them or their property without a good reason. If they are arrested, they must be read their rights, and they have the right to remain silent and to talk to a lawyer.

The Juvenile Courts

Most young people's cases are heard in juvenile courts. These courts were created around 1900 to rehabilitate young people and help them to stop from misbehaving, not to punish them. The proceedings in juvenile court are called hearings, not trials; they are held in private; and there is no jury.

The state insists that parents owe certain duties to their children. These include the responsibility of sending their children to school. Some parents, however, prefer to teach their children at home, so the states have created laws about home-schooling to guide them.

Instead of being found guilty, juveniles are determined to be delinquent, and the judge makes a disposition, rather than sentencing them. The judge is supposed to do what is in the best interests of the child, rather than to give out punishment. Every state has rules protecting the privacy of minors. In some states, juvenile court records are kept confidential; in others, they are sealed; and in a few, they are destroyed once the person reaches 18.

The Youngest Killers

Children as young as 10 have been tried for murder. In one case, two boys, aged 12 and 13, killed a five-year-old by dropping him out of a l4th-story window in Chicago because he would not steal candy for them. They were tried in the juvenile system, but later, Illinois law was changed to allow similar cases to be tried in adult court. In Britain, two 10-year-old boys, John Venables and Robert Thompson (pictured), were tried in adult court for the murder of two-year-old James Bulger. Their names and photographs were published in the paper during the trial. After they were found guilty, they were sentenced to a maximum-security juvenile prison. When they turned 18, their sentence ended and they were given new identities. Judges ruled that the media could not report their whereabouts.

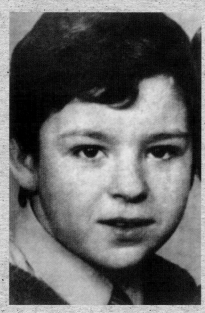

Far-Reaching Consequences

A juvenile record is not always kept secret, and if it becomes known, it can have life-changing consequences. When she was 13, Gina Grant was found by a juvenile court to have killed her violent, alcoholic mother. Some years later, she was accepted to Harvard University after completing her probation and finishing high school with high grades. But Harvard found out about her juvenile conviction and decided not to accept her, because they said that she had been dishonest by not telling them about her juvenile record on her application. Gina was later accepted at another college.

Colleges, employers, and the press cannot ever have access to these records, but government agencies, like the state police and the FBI, can look at them. If he or she commits a similar offense later as an adult, the judge can look at this juvenile record during sentencing.

If the child is found guilty and the offense is not too severe, the judge may choose a punishment that requires the child to follow certain rules, such as staying in school, obeying a curfew, paying for any damage, staying off drugs, doing community service, or getting a job. The juvenile probation officer makes sure that the young person sticks to these rules by making regular checks on him or her. If he or she does not, if the child has been in trouble before, or if the offense was quite serious, the child will be sent to a juvenile detention center.

Most states have a number of different juvenile detention centers, and the judge tries to send the child to the right one. Some are almost like prisons, because they house children who have committed serious offenses. Others allow residents to come and go because they have committed less serious offenses and are not likely to be dangerous.

Parental Duties

Parents have certain duties to their children. With rare exceptions, they have to support them until they are 18 or 21, depending on the age of majority in the state they live in. Parents can be held responsible for their children's actions. Some states have passed parental responsibility acts, allowing them to be **fined** if they do not stop a child from committing criminal offenses. So, for example, if parents know their child is out spray-painting graffiti every night, but do nothing to stop it, a judge might fine them.

Parents must send their children to school from the age of five or six until age 14 or 16, depending on the laws in the state. They also have to make sure that a child sees a doctor if he or she is really sick.

Children's Rights

There are laws protecting children from physical and sexual abuse, as well as neglect. Neglect means not taking proper care of children, such as by not taking care of them, feeding, or clothing them properly. If parents abuse or neglect their children, the state intervenes. Sometimes, the judge orders therapy, but if that does not work or if the problem is severe, the children can be taken away from their parents and sent into foster care temporarily, or even adopted by another family, if parental rights are terminated.

Divorce and Custody

Divorce is a civil suit in which one partner sues the other to end the marriage. The divorce separates the couple financially, dividing up any property and sometimes making provision for one spouse to give the other money to live on for a number of years. This is called alimony.

Custody of any children under 18 is also arranged during the divorce, as is child support. Although family courts try to get parents to work together to come to an agreement about what to do, sometimes compromise is impossible. Then the courts hold a custody hearing to hear testimony about each side's suitability to have physical and legal custody. The children are sometimes asked what they think. When the court has heard both sides, it decides what is best for the children.

A Brief History of Juvenile Justice

Until 1800, children over seven years old were tried and sentenced as adults. Some children as young as 12 were sentenced to death. In the 1800s, people began to change the way they thought about children and crime. They came to believe that young people needed rehabilitation, not punishment. In 1899, Illinois raised the age of criminal responsibility to 16 and set up the first juvenile court system. Over the next few years, the rest of the states set up similar courts under different names, including domestic relations court and family court.

If the parents get along well, they might decide on joint custody, a system in which they share the physical and legal custody of the children.

Child Support

After the divorce, money is often a problem. Many mothers and fathers are reluctant to keep up their child support payments. This can mean that the children suffer because the parent who has custody may not have enough for the family to live on. The federal Family Support Act requires all states to allow child support to be taken directly from someone's paycheck if he or she is not making child support payments voluntarily.

Even if two people who are not married have a child, the support rules are the same. Both the father and the mother are responsible for supporting their child.

A police officer talks with two sisters on his beat: this sort of informal contact is essential to achieve good community policing. To be effective in their jobs, it is important that police officers know their communities well.

Text-Dependent Questions

1. What cases are heard by juvenile courts?
2. What duties do parents owe their children?
3. What is custody?

Research Projects

1. Find some cases of serious crimes committed by very young people, such as the murder of two-year-old James Bulger by 10-year-olds John Venables and Robert Thompson. Should children who commit serious crimes be tried and imprisoned as adults?
2. What happens to juveniles convicted of crimes in your state? How do these young people turn out as adults?
3. How do courts generally handle custody in your state? How do they allocate child support? How do courts ensure that child support is actually paid?

SERIES GLOSSARY

Amnesty: pardon given by a country to citizens who have committed crimes

Anarchist: a person who wants to do away with organized society and government

Antiglobalization: against large companies or economies spreading into other nations

Appeal: referral of a case to a higher court for review

Arraignment: a formal court hearing at which the prisoner is asked whether he or she pleads "guilty" or "not guilty" to the charge or charges

Bifurcated: divided into two branches or parts

Bioassay: chemical analysis of biological samples

Biometrics: use of physical characteristics, such as fingerprints and voice, to identify users

Certificate of certiorari: a document that a losing party files with the Supreme Court, asking the Supreme Court to review the decision of a lower court; it includes a list of the parties, a statement of the facts of the case, and arguments as to why the court should grant the writ

Circumstantial evidence: evidence that can contribute to the conviction of an accused person but that is not considered sufficient without eyewitness or forensic evidence

Civil disobedience: refusing, in a peaceful way, to obey a government policy or law

Clemency: an act of leniency or mercy, especially to moderate the severity of punishment due

Commute: to change a penalty to another one less severe

Cryptology: the science and art of making and breaking codes and ciphers

Dactylography: the original name for the taking and analysis of fingerprints

Deputy: a person appointed as a substitute with power to act

Dissident: someone who disagrees with an established religious or political system, organization, or belief

Distributed Denial of Service (DDOS) attack: a malware attack that floods all the bandwidth of a system or server, causing the system to be unable to service real business

Effigy: a model or dummy of someone

Electronic tagging: the attaching of an electronic device to a criminal after he or she has been released, in order to track the person to ensure that he or she does not commit a crime again

Ethics: the discipline dealing with what is good and bad and with moral duty and obligation

Euthanasia: the act of killing or permitting the death of hopelessly sick or injured individuals in a relatively painless way for reasons of mercy

Exhume: to dig up a corpse, usually for examination

Exoneration: a finding that a person is not in fact guilty of the crime for which he or she has been accused

Extortion: the act of obtaining money from a person by force, intimidation, or undue or illegal power

Forensics: the scientific analysis and review of the physical and medical evidence of a crime

Garrote: to strangle someone using a thin wire with handles at either end

Gibbet: an upright post with a projecting arm for hanging the bodies of executed criminals as a warning

Graft: the acquisition of gain (as money) in dishonest or questionable ways

Grievance: a real or imagined wrong, for which there are thought to be reasonable grounds for complaint

Heresy: religious convictions contrary to church dogma and that deviate from orthodox belief

Hulk: a ship used as a prison

Hypostasis: the migration of blood to the lowest parts of a dead body, caused by the effect of gravity

Incendiary: a bomb

Infiltrate: to enter or become established in gradually or unobtrusively, usually for subversive purposes

Intern (v.): to confine or impound, especially during a war

Interpol: an association of national police forces that promotes cooperation and mutual assistance in apprehending international criminals and criminals who flee abroad to avoid justice

Intrusion detection system (IDS): software designed to detect misuse of a system

Junta: a group of military officers who hold power, usually as the result of a coup

Jurisprudence: a system or body of law

Ladder: an early form of the rack in which the victim was tied to a vertical framework and weights were attached to his ankles

Lag: a convict

Latent: present and capable of becoming obvious, or active, even though not currently visible

Lockstep: a mode of marching in step where people move one after another as closely as possible

Lynch: to attack and kill a person, typically by hanging, without involvement of the courts or legal system and often done by a mob

Manifesto: a written statement declaring publicly the intentions, motives, or views of its issuer

Manslaughter: the unlawful killing of a human being without express or implied intent

Martyrdom: the suffering of death on account of adherence to a cause and especially to one's religious faith

Mercenary: a man or woman who is paid by a foreign government or organization to fight in its service

Miscreant: one who behaves criminally or viciously

Molotov cocktail: an explosive weapon; each "cocktail" is a bottle filled with gasoline and wrapped in a rag or plugged with a wick, then ignited and thrown

Money laundering: to transfer illegally obtained money through an outside party to conceal the true source

Mule: a person who smuggles drugs inside his or her body

Mutinous: to resist lawful authority

Paramilitary: of, relating to, being, or characteristic of a force formed on a military pattern, especially as a potential auxiliary military force

Pathologist: a physician who specializes in examining tissue samples and fluids to diagnose diseases

PCR: polymerase chain reaction, a technique of making multiple copies of a small section of DNA so that it can be analyzed and identified

Personal alarm: a small electronic device that a person can carry and activate if he or she feels threatened

Phreaker: a person who hacks telephone systems

Pillory: a device formerly used for publicly punishing offenders consisting of a wooden frame with holes in which the head and hands can be locked

Political asylum: permitting foreigners to settle in your country to escape danger in another country, usually his or her native land

Postmortem: an autopsy; an examination of a dead body, looking for causes of death

Precedent: something done or said that serves as an example or rule to authorize or justify a subsequent act of similar kind

Pyramid scheme: an investment swindle in which some early investors are paid off with money put up by later ones in order to encourage more and bigger risks; also called a Ponzi scheme

Quick: the living flesh beneath the fingernails

Racketeering: the act of conducting a fraudulent scheme or activity

Ratchet: a mechanism consisting of a "pawl," a hinged catch that slips into sloping teeth of a cogwheel, so that it can be turned only in one direction

Repatriation: returning a person to his or her country of origin

Ruse: a subterfuge in order to distract someone's attention

Screw: slang term for a prison guard

Scuttle: to cut a hole through the bottom, deck, or side of a ship

Seditious: of, relating to, or tending toward an incitement of resistance to or insurrection against lawful authority

Serology: the laboratory analysis of blood serum, particularly in the detection of blood groups and antibodies

Siege (n.): a standoff situation, in which a group holds a position by force and refuses to surrender

Slander: a false and defamatory oral statement about a person

Smash and grab: a term used to describe a method of stealing, where thieves break windows (for example, on a shop front or a car) to grab the goods within before fleeing

Statute: a law enacted by the legislative branch of a government

Statutory: authorized by the statute that defines the law

Subversive: characterized by systematic attempts to overthrow or undermine a government or political system by persons working secretly from within

Succinylcholine: a synthetic drug that paralyzes muscle fiber

Vendetta: an often-prolonged series of retaliatory, vengeful, or hostile acts or exchange of such acts

White-collar crime: crime committed by office staff, usually involving theft from the company they work for

Worm: a computer program that enters one computer and replicates itself to spread to other computers; unlike a virus, it does not have to attach itself to other files

Xenophobic: having an unreasonable fear of what is foreign and especially of people of foreign origin

CHRONOLOGY

1775–1783: Revolutionary War.

1776: Declaration of Independence is signed.

1787: Constitutional Convention takes place in Philadelphia, Pennsylvania; December 7, Delaware becomes the first state to ratify the Constitution.

1790: May 29, Rhode Island becomes the last state to ratify the Constitution.

1791: December 15, Bill of Rights ratified.

1795: Amendment 11 ratified, defining the judicial power of the United States.

1803: February 24, *Marbury v. Madison* decision creates principle of judicial review.

1856: *Scott v. Sandford*: Dred Scott, a slave, sued for his freedom, but the Supreme Court dismissed the suit, ruling that as a slave Scott was not a citizen and also that his owner's property rights were protected by the Constitution.

1868: July 9, 14th Amendment is ratified, giving citizens in all states equal protection under the law.

1908: FBI is established.

1913: Amendment 16 ratified, establishing Congress' power to collect taxes; Amendment 17 ratified, establishing direct election of the Senate by the voters.

1919: Amendment 18 ratified, establishing Prohibition, which forbade the sale of intoxicating liquors.

1920: Amendment 19 ratified, giving women the right to vote.

1932: *Powell v. Alabama*: the Court ruled that defendants had a right to a lawyer when they were being tried for an offense punishable with the death penalty (Ozie Powell was one of the Scottsboro Boys).

1933: Amendment 20 ratified, known as the lame duck amendment, reducing time between presidential election and inauguration; Amendment 21 ratified, repealing Prohibition.

1951:	Amendment 22 ratified, restricting presidents to two terms.
1954:	*Brown v. Board of Education*: the Court put an end to the separate but equal doctrine, saying "In the field of public education the doctrine of 'separate but equal' has no place. Separate educational facilities are inherently unequal."
1958:	*NAACP v. Alabama*: the right to assemble in groups was protected by the Court's decision in this case.
1961:	Amendment 23 ratified, giving residents of the District of Columbia the right to vote in presidential elections.
1963:	*Abington School District v. Schempp*: the Court found that saying prayers in school was a violation of the First Amendment right to freedom of religion.
1966:	*Miranda v. Arizona*: the Court ruled that anyone accused of a crime had to be informed of his or her constitutional rights, such as the right to remain silent and the right to a lawyer.
1967:	Amendment 25 ratified, clarifying presidential succession.
1971:	Amendment 26 ratified, giving the right to vote to 18-year-olds.
1973:	*Roe v. Wade*: this case effectively legalized abortion.
1992:	27th Amendment ratified.
1993:	World Trade Center bombing.
1995:	Oklahoma City bombing destroys Alfred P. Murrah Federal Building. Bomber Timothy McVeigh sentenced to death and executed in 2001.
2000:	U.S. Supreme Court decides 2000 Presidential election in favour of George Bush in its decision *Bush v. Gore*.
2001:	September 11 terrorist attacks on World Trade Center and Pentagon.
2012:	Trayvon Martin, a black teenager, shot and killed by a white neighbor. Florida's courts find Zimmerman innocent of murder.
2014:	Michael Brown, a black man, shot by white police officer in Ferguson, Missouri, sparking accusations of police brutality and riots between African Americans and the police force.

FURTHER INFORMATION

Useful Web Sites

American Bar Association: www.abanet.org

Center on Juvenile and Criminal Justice: www.cjcj.org

Federal Bureau of Investigation (FBI): www.fbi.gov

Opinions and resources on the Supreme Court and other cases: www.findlaw
.com

United States Courts: www.uscourts.gov

United States Department of Justice: www.justice.gov

Further Reading

Boland, Mary L. *Crime Victim's Guide to Justice*. Napeville, IL: Sourcebooks.
1997.

Calvi, James V. and Susan Coleman. *American Law and Legal Systems*.
Englewood Cliffs, NJ: Prentice Hall, 1989.

Cole, George, et al. *The American System of Criminal Justice*. Wadsworth
Publishing, 2014.

Deneberger, Barry. *The True Story of J. Edgar Hoover and the FBI*. New York,
Scholastic, 1993.

Durrett, Deanne. *Teen Privacy Rights–A Hot Issue*. Berkley Heights, NJ:
Enslow Publishers Inc., 2001.

Graham, Robert. *Crime Fighting*. Austin, Texas: Raintree Stech-Vaughn, 1995.

Irving, Shae and Kathleen Michon (eds.). *Nolo's Encyclopedia of Everyday
Law: Answers to Your Most Frequently Asked Legal Questions*. Berkeley,
Ca: Nolo Press, 2002.

Neubauer, David, and Henry Fradella. *America's Courts and the Criminal
Justice System*. Wadsworth Publishing, 2013.

Van Wormer, Katherine, and Clemens Bartollas. *Women and the Criminal
Justice System*. New York: Prentice Hall, 2013.

About the Author

Ellen Dupont has written on a wide variety of subjects, mostly for publishers of illustrated books, such as Reader's Digest, Time-Life Books, Dorling Kindersley Books, and Grolier. Having edited several health books, Ellen began writing on health and has either contributed to or ghostwritten a number of health titles. In addition to general consumer health subjects, Ellen specializes in food and nutrition. She has run children's cooking classes and adapted recipes from around the world for children.

Ellen has written three books on consumer rights and the law: *The U.S. Judicial System, Criminal Terminology*, and *Fair Recruitment and Selection*. The first two were written for young adults and explain the principles and practice of the American legal system to high school students. *Fair Recruitment and Selection* is a guide for managers covering equal opportunities policies, creating a job specification, interviewing and assessment, and candidate selection. Other topics that Ellen has written on are the paranormal, mythology, movie stars, and pets.

A native of Connecticut and a graduate of Brown University, Ellen lives in London, England, with her husband and son.

INDEX

PICTURE CREDITS